CW00448739

Exploiting People for Profit

Simon Massey • Glynn Rankin

Exploiting People for Profit

Trafficking in Human Beings

palgrave
macmillan

Simon Massey
Faculty of Arts and Humanities
Coventry University
Coventry, UK

Glynn Rankin
Liverpool John Moores University
Liverpool, UK

ISBN 978-1-137-43412-8   ISBN 978-1-137-43413-5   (eBook)
https://doi.org/10.1057/978-1-137-43413-5

This Palgrave Pivot imprint is published by the registered company Springer Nature Limited.
The registered company address is: The Campus, 4 Crinan Street, London, N1 9XW, United Kingdom

Contents

About the Authors

Simon Massey is a senior lecturer at Coventry University, UK, where he is the director for two postgraduate courses in the School of Humanities. Amongst his research interests is irregular migration from Africa to Europe. He is co-editor with Rino Coluccello of *Eurafrican Migration: Legal, Economic and Social Responses to Irregular Migration* (Palgrave Macmillan, 2015) and has published scholarly articles on the criminal networks and mechanisms involved in human trafficking and people smuggling. He has also worked as a consultant for the EU and the UNDP.

Glynn Rankin was called to the bar by Middle Temple in 1983. He was a prosecutor for over 20 years, holding a number of senior positions with the Crown Prosecution Service where he became an acknowledged expert in the combatting of human trafficking both in the UK and in the international arena. He was also a co-founder of the UK Human Trafficking Centre.

He has considerable experience in the prosecution of immigration crime, human trafficking, people smuggling, labour exploitation and passport and identity offences. He advises government and intergovernmental organisations on policy, law and strategy firmly based on an ethical and human rights approach. He is an independent expert who provides strategic and practical expertise in the area of human trafficking.

List of Boxes

Introduction

Human trafficking permeates seemingly routine aspects of everyday life. Even in a country such as the United Kingdom (UK) that considers itself alert to the threat, instances of human trafficking occur in plain sight. In 2016, a 'slave workforce' made up of trafficked Hungarian workers was discovered in a bed-making factory in Yorkshire. The owner was found to be paying his workforce just £10 each week whilst accommodating them in squalid conditions. Despite a requirement under the Modern Slavery Act (2015) for companies to audit their supply chains, major high street retailers continued to sell the beds without scrutinising the conditions in which they were being made. In 2019, an organised criminal gang was found guilty of trafficking over 400 persons, mainly vulnerable addicts or ex-convicts, from Poland to the West Midlands in order to supply low-skilled workers to well-known companies and high street supermarket chains. The victims were isolated, threatened and accommodated in cramped and filthy conditions, and their wages sequestered by their traffickers.

Human trafficking is a fundamental violation of human rights and one of the most serious crimes. It takes many forms and affects people of all ages, genders and races. Other terms are sometimes used to describe the same crime including Trafficking in Human Beings (THB) and Trafficking in Persons (TIP). For consistency, this book will use the term 'human trafficking', a complex transnational phenomenon brought about by interrelated economic, social, cultural, political and personal factors. More recently, the term and concept of 'modern slavery' has increasingly replaced 'human trafficking' as a more comprehensive 'umbrella' descriptor encompassing a spectrum of exploitative criminal activity. This trend and the distinction between these terms and concepts are assessed in the first chapter. However, whilst reference to modern slavery and data connected to modern slavery is inescapable, notably in the UK where the crime of human trafficking has been subsumed in statute law by the more extensive crime of modern slavery, this book will focus on the socio-legal dimensions of the narrower concept of human trafficking.

This short book provides a succinct, critical evaluation of the current status of strategies to counter the crime of human trafficking, based on the authors' experience of current counter-trafficking practice. It aims to synthesise causality, criminality, victimhood, impact and counter-trafficking strategy, making current socio-legal thinking on human trafficking accessible to an academic, practitioner and general readership. Co-authored by a legal practitioner and an academic, the intent is to correlate the practical and the academic approach to countering human trafficking, to give the reader an informed appreciation of what human trafficking means at the present time, as well as an insight into the scholarly criticism of the strategic response to it. Drawing on the respective occupational backgrounds of the authors, the broad approach taken to this study is that of socio-legal studies. As a multi-discipline 'methodology', socio-legal analysis 'provides theories, concepts, testable hypotheses and robust empirical findings to understand the inter-action of laws, legal actors…and legal institutions with the people and other institutions that are affected by law' (Menkel-Meadow 2020).

A first chapter seeks to place human trafficking in its social and legal contexts, briefly exploring how individuals and sections of society become susceptible to the inducements of traffickers, as well as ascertaining the shape and scale of the current threat. The bulk of the chapter seeks to provide, if not a conclusive definition, then an evaluative overview of how the crime is delineated by core international legislation. Finally, it considers, with particular emphasis on new domestic legislation in the UK and Australia, the relationship between human trafficking and modern-day slavery.

The second chapter investigates two core variables in determining whether the crime of human trafficking has occurred. Firstly, the importance of agency and consent are core distinguishing factors in differentiating between the related, but distinct, crimes of human trafficking and smuggling of persons. This distinction underpins the immigration regimes of individual states and supra-national entities, notably the EU. The crisis that has played out on the maritime borders of Europe in recent years has, in many ways, resulted from the decision to treat the majority of migrants as smuggled, and therefore illegal immigrants, rather than trafficked, and therefore victims. The second part of the chapter focuses on the nature of exploitation as the fundamental purpose of trafficking, exploring definitional ambiguities, as well as the practical problems faced by investigators and prosecutors in locating the boundary between mistreatment and criminal exploitation given the current expansion and recognition of an increasing number of forms of exploitation.

The three following chapters are based on the 'four Ps' counter-trafficking framework: pursuit, protection, prevention and partnership (Winterdyk 2018: 113–114). Whilst the last of these counter-methodologies is not assigned a discrete chapter, the fundamental necessity for partnerships— between law enforcement and criminal justice agencies, between states, between the public and private sectors—to effectively counter the threat of human is stressed throughout the book.

The third chapter focuses on the pursuit of traffickers by exploring the related challenges of investigating and prosecuting cases of human trafficking. In particular, it considers the benefits and disadvantages of specialist techniques, often involving the invasion of privacy, developed to investigate a complex and frequently transnational crime. Investigating cases that cross multiple borders necessitates law enforcement and criminal justice agencies working closely together. The second part of the chapter concentrates on partnership as a prerequisite for the pursuit of traffickers, in particular assessing the effective and sophisticated mechanisms and institutions developed by the EU to facilitate both the investigation and prosecution of trafficking cases. A final section considers the likely consequences of Britain's withdrawal from the EU on the future capacity of the UK and EU authorities to effectively catch and convict those involved in trafficking.

The fourth chapter focuses on the victim. Often severely damaged, both physically and psychologically, victims are also forced into committing criminal acts and can be arrested and punished despite the existence of legal measures to prevent the prosecution of trafficked victims. Indeed, although victims ostensibly should be protected by a spectrum of rights under internationals law, the application of these rights varies according to jurisdiction. This particularly applies to the variable protection offered by each jurisdiction's national referral mechanisms (NRM). The role of NRMs is investigated in the final section of the chapter.

The final chapter assesses the status of prevention as a strategy to address human trafficking. Substantial resources have been dedicated by international organisations and national governments to prevent trafficking before it happens. Yet, these disparate 'projects' have historically often suffered from inadequate and unscientific evaluation. As the quality and consistency of evaluation has improved, there is growing evidence that some of the most widespread strategies used to prevent trafficking are either ineffective or unhelpful.

References

Menkel-Meadow, C., (2020), 'Uses and Abuses of Socio-Legal Studies' in Creutzfeldt, N., Mason, M., and McConnachie, K. (eds.), *Routledge Handbook of Socio-Legal Theory and Methods*. Abingdon: Routledge.
Winterdyk, J., (2018), 'Combating (child) human trafficking: building capacity', *Oñati Sociolegal Series*, Vol. 8, No. 1.

1

Human Trafficking in Context

Abstract The chapter puts the crime, and concept, of human trafficking in context. Human trafficking is caused by a variety of cultural and economic drivers, including push factors such as gender and social discrimination, poverty and the absence of employment opportunities. Whilst data on the prevalence of human trafficking remains inconsistent, it is clear that the crime poses a serious threat that is most likely under-estimated in the existing statistics. International law, notably the UN Trafficking Protocol, stipulates that the offence should be dealt with as a process comprised of three constituent elements—action, means and purpose. However, increasing variation in the way in which the crime is framed in domestic law, especially the shift in the UK towards the broader offence of modern slavery, has the potential to dilute human trafficking as a stand-alone offence.

Keywords: Push-factors • Prevalence • Process • Constituent elements • Modern slavery

The criminality involved in human trafficking is as varied as it is brutal: abduction, incarceration, rape, sexual enslavement, enforced prostitution, forced labour, removal of organs for transplant, physical beatings, starvation

© The Author(s) 2020
S. Massey, G. Rankin, *Exploiting People for Profit*,
https://doi.org/10.1057/978-1-137-43413-5_1

and the denial of medical treatment are activities correlated with the overarching crime of human trafficking. A prerequisite to effectively countering this criminality is an understanding of how this relatively new crime has been framed by core international organisations.

International law, which derives from several sources including international conventions and treaties, as well as from customary law, is the body of law that acts out the legal relationship between states. The definition of human trafficking derives from international law, and international legal developments continue to influence the way in which individual states address human trafficking at national level. The 2018 edition of the *Global Report on Trafficking in Persons* published by United Nations Office on Drugs and Crime (UNODC) indicates that 'the data show that victims who have been detected within their own national borders now represent the largest part of the victims detected worldwide' (UNODC 2018: 13). The *Global Report*, nonetheless, also recognises that 'transnational trafficking networks are still prevalent and must be responded to through international cooperation' (UNODC 2018: 13). Given that human trafficking was only defined in international law in 2000, there is a debate over whether it is a new phenomenon in terms of methods, mechanisms, criminality and victims, or whether it is a continuation of existing forms of exploitation, usually described as slavery, exacerbated by the pressures and tensions of globalisation.

The broadly accepted position amongst academics and practitioners is that most human trafficking is committed within established models of transnational organised crime (Salt and Stein 1997; Shelley 2007; Aronowitz 2017). However, in a significant number of cases, the organised groups involved are operating within networks based on family, kin and community. This activity may be within state boundaries or over porous borders within ethnic nations where history and culture act, alongside financial gain, as potent motivations. There is evidence that traffickers operate according to different criminal models dependent on differing circumstances, including the hierarchical model, loose criminal networks and the market model of transnational crime. Equally, there are indications that those involved with human trafficking can also be involved in other illegal activities including people smuggling, drug and arms trafficking, money laundering and, in some cases, terrorism. There is also evidence of overlap between illicit and licit activity; for example, there is often a thin line between exploitative pay and working conditions that constitute human trafficking in some state jurisdictions, and low pay and poor working conditions that fall short of the crime of human trafficking in other jurisdictions. In this regard, corruption on the part of local and national authorities is often a prerequisite for profitable trafficking.

The purpose of this first chapter is to place the crime, and concept, of human trafficking in context. It is divided into four sections. The first section delineates the broad causal factors that lead to people becoming susceptible to trafficking. Secondly, the chapter seeks to establish the seriousness of human trafficking as a contemporary threat to human security. Thirdly, the chapter surveys the boundaries of the concept 'human trafficking' with reference to core international legislation passed by the United Nations, Council of Europe and the European Union. Finally, the concept of 'human trafficking' is distinguished from the increasingly prevalent use of the term 'modern slavery'.

Root Causes

Human trafficking is a highly profitable crime based on the principles of supply and demand, which exploit push and pull factors in the states of origin and destination. There is an abundant supply of victims within the states of origin and a growing demand for the services of the victims in the states of destination, creating the ideal business environment for the traffickers. Many of the drivers of human trafficking are specific to individual trafficking patterns and to the states in which they occur. There are, however, factors that are common to human trafficking in general or found in a wide range of different regions, patterns or cases. These can include socio-cultural factors such as family or peer pressure, a patriarchal family structure, gender discrimination, social discrimination, states or regions where women are the sole providers, poor education, as well as cultural practices. Economic factors include disparity in wealth distribution, poverty, a shortage of employment opportunities and the desire to improve living standards. These conditions are often prevalent in states undergoing rapid economic transition, for example, states from the former Soviet space or the expanding economies of West and East Africa. Political factors can include government policies and conflict.

These influences create the push factors which foster acquiescence to, what otherwise might be seen as unsafe, offers of help to travel or find work abroad. Arguably, these push factors instil a vulnerability in potential trafficking victims that can be exploited by traffickers who manipulate the pull factors of job opportunities: higher salaries, improved living and welfare standards, and the intangible enticement of a 'better life'. A study of human trafficking in Europe and Eurasia by USAID found that nearly 80% of male victims of trafficking assisted by International Organisation for Migration (IOM) in Ukraine cited 'a desire to improve their living conditions as their main reason for migrating' (USAID 2010: 12). Cecilia Mo argues that the vulnerability that results from deprivation can involve an increase in risk-seeking that leads to a greater chance of exploitation (2018).

> While improving awareness, legal protections and enforcement are certainly important, in considering policy levers to combat human trafficking, it is important to consider how potentially vulnerable individuals make decisions. Informing families about human trafficking is insufficient if they are willing to accept the risk of being exploited given a potential upside e.g., a better job. (Mo 2018: 271)

However, the concept of vulnerability in the context of human trafficking remains under-researched, and the lack of data impedes comprehensive understanding of the interplay between divergent vulnerabilities and their cumulative and intersectional effects.

Vulnerability to trafficking and to different forms of exploitation is shaped by gender. The EU Strategy towards the Eradication of Trafficking in Human Beings (2012–2016), referred to in this book as the EU Strategy, asserts that

> while women and girls tend to be trafficked for exploitation in the sex industry, in domestic work or the care sector, men and boys tend to be victims of forced labour, in particular in agriculture, construction, mining, forestry sectors and on fishing fleets. In addition, the short and long term consequences on trafficked women and men might differ, depending on the form of trafficking and gender. (2012: 13)

A Eurostat working paper published in February 2015 collates data from across member states that measure registered trafficking victims. Recognising that women and men can be trafficked for a variety of exploitative purposes, Eurostat, nonetheless, reports that

> of all the female victims registered, the overwhelming majority were trafficked for the purpose of sexual exploitation (85%). Among registered male victims, 64% were trafficked for labour exploitation. A distinct gender split can also be seen within the different types of exploitation. Registered victims of sexual exploitation are predominantly female (95%) whereas the majority of registered victims of labour exploitation are male (71%). (2015: 11)

There is evidence that a policy response that emphasises restricting immigration can increase migrant vulnerability and facilitate abuse. For example, in the context of the 'restrictive and complex workings of the UK immigration system', Peter Dwyer et al. argue that 'migrants, fearful of deportation and with limited understanding of their rights, are coerced or threatened into forced labour' (2011: 29). Human trafficking is, in its modern form, a phenomenon that is inextricably linked to, and shaped by, the dynamics of contemporary global migration (Danziger et al. 2009). Severely restricted immigration policies are more likely to fuel organised, irregular migration than stop the movement of people, and the tightening of immigration policies in many destination states has led to a decrease in the legal opportunities for international migration, creating an environment that is conducive to migrant smuggling (Bosco et al. 2009). A further corollary to a restrictive immigration policy concerns the impact of such a policy on the access of victims to welfare services. A study undertaken by Ieke de Vries et al. concludes that whilst 'the American public shares deep concerns about human trafficking...those who possess stronger anti-immigrant sentiment...tend to be less supportive of services directed at the protection of migrant trafficked persons (2019: 140).

Human trafficking is a market-driven criminal industry, with consumers willing to pay a specific price for goods and services. Dita Vogel argues that 'demand is often not defined at all in anti-trafficking debates' (2015:

34). For Vogel, the term 'demand' in the context of human trafficking should be used in the sense adopted by the discipline of economics, a 'willingness and ability to buy a particular commodity' (Vogel 2015: 34). Traffickers rely upon consumers failing to identify, or ignoring, human trafficking. Hence, traffickers offer otherwise unavailable or illegal services, or provide cheaper services and labour. Whilst, typically, labour exploitation is driven by ruthless employers at the end of the trafficking chain across a range of different sectors, exploitation can also result from the actions of brokers or agents, or from multiple individuals involved in trafficking networks at junctures along the trafficking process (ICAT 2014; Massari 2015).

Counter-trafficking policies, and concomitant law enforcement and criminal justice responses, have tended to target the supply side of the phenomenon. This, despite Article 6 of the Council of Europe Convention on Action against Human Trafficking, referred to in this book as the CoE Convention, explicitly requires states to respond to the demand for the products of exploitation (see Box 5.1). Yet, on the whole, the demand for exploited persons across all forms of human trafficking has attracted less prominence in national policy-making. In the context of labour exploitation, the Inter-Agency Coordination Group against Trafficking in Persons (ICAT), an inter-agency forum mandated by the UN General Assembly to advise on an holistic approach to countering human trafficking, makes a series of recommendations. ICAT advises an increased focus on the demand side at the national level by criminal justice agencies, improved regulation of labour standards, a reduction in exploitative migration practices, more transparent monitoring of supply chains, and encouraging consumer awareness and action against products made by trafficking victims. In particular, ICAT warns that

> trafficking is more likely to occur where there is social exclusion of, or discrimination against, certain groups, affecting the willingness of employers and other agents to exploit them, the willingness of society to tolerate such practices and the willingness of the government, in particular law enforcement, to respond appropriately. (ICAT 2014: 27)

Is Human Trafficking a Problem?

Accurate statistics measuring the extent of human trafficking are notoriously ambiguous and inconsistent. Adopting the broader categorisation of 'modern slavery', the International Labour Organisation (ILO) and Walk Free Foundation (WFF) estimate that at any given time in 2016, there were an estimated 40.3 million people in modern slavery, including 24.9 million in forced labour and 15.4 million in forced marriage (2017). The ILO estimates that of the 24.9 million in forced labour, 16 million are exploited in the private sector in domestic servitude in construction or agriculture, 4.8 million are in forced sexual exploitation and 4 million people are in forced labour imposed by the state (2017). The use of the expanded descriptor 'modern slavery' rather than human trafficking is controversial, and the distinction between these two terms and concepts is discussed later in this chapter.

Eurostat, tasked with analysing human trafficking within the EU, recognises that 'measuring trafficking in human beings across countries is a challenging task with many layers of complexity' (Eurostat 2015: 14). Eurostat has sought to improve the quality of the available data through validation checks and improved definitions. However, the statistics are restricted to those human trafficking cases that come to the attention of the authorities in the EU member states, together with the European Free Trade Association (EFTA), European Economic Area (EEA) and EU candidate countries Iceland, Montenegro, Norway, Serbia, Switzerland and Turkey. The extent to which human trafficking is prioritised by criminal justice and law enforcement agencies in these states varies, as does the rigour of data collection and statistical collation. The ultimate utility of Eurostat's data in the area of human trafficking should be judged in the light of these limitations.

The Eurostat figures indicate that 30,146 victims were registered by EU states between 2010 and 2012. Of these, 80% were female. A substantial majority, 69%, were trafficked for sexual exploitation, of which 95% were female. Over 1000 children were registered as victims of sexual exploitation. Conversely, 71% of victims of labour exploitation were male. In terms of the geographical region of origin, 65% of victims were citizens of

EU member states. Measuring the criminal justice response to human trafficking, Eurostat totalled 8805 prosecutions between 2010 and 2012, of which 70% involved male victims. Over the same period, 3855 traffickers were convicted (Eurostat 2015). More recently, Eurostat reports the number of registered victims of human trafficking in the EU in the single year of 2016 to be 11,385, whilst the number in 2015 was 9147, making a total of 20,532 in the period 2015–2016. Eurostat, however, cautions that the data is possibly skewed by one large member state, with France providing data only from 2016 (Eurostat 2018: 34–35). Based on a registered victim prevalence rate formula, the nationalities most likely to be registered as victims both in their own country and in other member states are Bulgarian, Latvian and Romanian, whilst the nationalities most likely to be registered as victims outside their own countries are Bulgarian and Romanian. For non-EU citizens, the top five nationalities of trafficking victims were Nigerian, Brazilian, Chinese, Vietnamese and Russian.

In the UK, 3800 victims of human trafficking had been formally identified by 2016. However, a Home Office estimate made in 2014 of about 13,000 victims was revised upward in August 2017 to the 'tens of thousands'. Will Kerr, the National Crime Agency's former Director of Vulnerabilities, states that

> the more we look for modern slavery the more we find evidence of the widespread abuse of the vulnerable. The growing body of evidence we are collecting points to the scale being far larger than anyone had previously thought. (*Guardian* 10 August 2017)

The 2018 Global Slavery Index estimates that in 2016, there were about 136,000 individuals living in modern slavery in the UK, a figure much higher than the government's own estimates (2018). The figure also greatly surpasses the numbers being referred to the UK's NRM, the framework for identifying and referring potential victims of human trafficking (see Chap. 4). In 2018, a total of 6993 potential victims were referred to the NRM, a 36% increase on the 2017 figure of 5142. In the third quarter of 2019, between 1 July and 30 September, 2808 potential victims were referred to the NRM, a 21% increase from the previous

Table 1.1 *Global law enforcement data: Total human trafficking prosecutions and convictions* (labour trafficking prosecutions and convictions in parentheses)

Year	Prosecutions	Convictions	Victims identified
2012	7705 (1153)	4746 (518)	46,570 (17,368)
2013	9460 (1199)	5776 (470)	44,758 (10,603)
2014	10,051 (418)	4443 (216)	44,462 (11,438)
2015	19,127 (857)	6615 (456)	77,823 (14,262)
2016	14,939 (1038)	9072 (717)	68,453 (17,465)
2017	17,471 (869)	7135 (332)	96,960 (23,906)
2018	11,096 (457)	7481 (259)	85,613 (11,009)

Source: US Department of State (2019), *Trafficking in Persons Report*. Washington, DC: US Dept of State Publications

quarter and a 61% increase from the same quarter in 2018. The largest number of referrals were from the UK, Albania and Vietnam, with the UK figure rising 100% from the previous year. Labour exploitation, including criminal exploitation, was the most common type of exploitation (NCA 2019: 1).

In recent years, the number of human trafficking prosecutions globally, as collated by the US' *Trafficking in Persons Report*, has increased (see Table 1.1). However, in comparison with the rising estimates of human trafficking in all regions of the world, prosecution lags behind the incidence of trafficking.

One reason for the relatively low level of prosecutions and convictions is the complexity of investigating human trafficking crimes, often requiring the concerted efforts of source, transit and destination countries, as well as a multi-agency approach that consumes considerable human and material resources and time. Being multidimensional, cases of human trafficking are more difficult to investigate and prosecute than most other crimes. Challenges linked to the prosecution of human trafficking cases include the identification of victims and networks, high evidentiary requirements with victim testimony being often difficult to obtain, and insufficient cross-border police and judicial cooperation. There is a tendency, for example, for national authorities to focus on the national dimension of any particular investigation. Links with criminal activity in other jurisdictions are sometimes not recognised, or recognised but disregarded.

What Is Human Trafficking?

Human trafficking is a fundamental violation of human rights. It is the third largest criminal enterprise in the world after the illegal sale of drugs and arms. The human rights of trafficked persons rest at the centre of all efforts to prevent and combat trafficking and to protect, assist and provide redress to victims. Anti-trafficking measures should not adversely affect the human rights and dignity of persons, especially the rights of those who have been trafficked. A human rights-based approach to countering human trafficking requires states to set up a comprehensive framework for the protection of trafficked persons as victims of a serious human rights violation based on the effective investigation and prosecution of traffickers.

The UN has played a core role in setting international human rights standards from which strategies and policies to combat human trafficking have been designed. International law on human trafficking derives from the United Nations Convention against Transnational Organised Crime (UNTOC). The first internationally recognised definition of human trafficking was in Article 3 of the United Nations Trafficking Protocol to Prevent, Suppress and Punish Human Trafficking, Especially Women and Children, referred to as the Trafficking Protocol. Those states that are a party to the UNTOC are also a party to the Trafficking Protocol, and the UNTOC and Trafficking Protocol should be interpreted together. The Trafficking Protocol is not a stand-alone tool. Rather, it supplements the UNTOC and is supported by an array of international legal instruments, some focusing on the suppression of crime and others on human rights (ICAT 2012).

For example, whilst international cooperation can be challenging due to legal, cultural, political and language issues, there exist rules and procedures to facilitate cooperation and legal tools to prosecute the traffickers. The UNTOC contains detailed provisions on both formal and informal cooperation in criminal matters, which are also applicable to the Trafficking Protocol. These include extradition (art. 16), transfer of sentenced persons (art. 17), mutual legal assistance (art. 18), joint investigations (art. 19), cooperation in using special investigative techniques (art.

20), transfer of criminal proceedings (art. 21), international cooperation for purposes of confiscation (art. 13–14) and law enforcement cooperation (art. 27).

Likewise, Article 15 of the UNTOC establishes a series of jurisdictional bases that are relevant to human trafficking cases. In this context, States Parties are obliged to provide for jurisdiction on the basis of the principle of territoriality (para. 1), as well as to establish extraterritorial jurisdiction for domestic prosecution in lieu of extradition when the latter is denied on the ground of nationality (para. 3). States Parties are further encouraged to establish jurisdiction on the basis of active and passive personality principles, namely, when their nationals are perpetrators or victims of related offences (para. 2), as well as establish jurisdiction for domestic prosecution in lieu of extradition when the latter is denied on grounds other than nationality (para. 4). The international legal rules on jurisdiction in trafficking situations are set out in major international and regional treaties. Their objective is to eliminate jurisdictional safe havens for traffickers by ensuring that all parts of the crime can be punished wherever an offence took place. Another concern is to ensure that coordination mechanisms are effective in cases where more than one state has grounds to assert jurisdiction. This is affirmed by the Association of South-East Asian Nations (ASEAN) which recognises 'that such cooperation is vital to successful domestic prosecutions'(ASEAN 2010: 1).

Human trafficking often has a truly international dimension, and investigations extend to other jurisdictions, requiring evidence for prosecutions to be obtained from abroad. Mutual Legal Assistance (MLA) is the principal mechanism for obtaining or exchanging information between different jurisdictions. MLA is applied for through a letter of request for assistance in obtaining specific evidence, detailed in the letter, for use in criminal proceedings or to support an investigation. The process is used to provide and obtain formal government-to-government assistance in criminal investigations and prosecutions. The exact type of MLA that states provide to one another is subject to national law and international arrangements (ASEAN 2010). Article 18 of UNTOC requires States Parties to afford one another the 'widest measure of mutual legal assistance in investigations, prosecutions and judicial proceedings' and to 'reciprocally extend to one another similar assistance where the requesting State Party has reasonable grounds to suspect that the offence…is transnational in nature, including that victims, witnesses, proceeds, instrumentalities or evidence of such offences are located in the requested State Party and that the offence involves an organised criminal group'.

The objective of the UNTOC is to promote international cooperation and combat transnational organised crime more effectively. It is supplemented by the Trafficking Protocol that commits ratifying states to preventing and combating human trafficking, protecting and assisting victims of trafficking and promoting cooperation among states in order to meet those objectives. It has been ratified by 174 States Parties. Human trafficking is increasingly accepted as a serious, and widespread, violation of human rights, and one of the principle objectives of international law is the protection of human rights. Yet, from its early days, the Trafficking Protocol has been criticised for focusing on criminal prosecution at the expense of the protection of the victims of human trafficking (Haynes 2007; Gallagher 2001).

The fundamental definition of human trafficking is supplied in an annex of the Trafficking Protocol (see Box 1.1).

Box 1.1   Definition of 'human trafficking'

(a) Human trafficking shall mean the recruitment, transportation, transfer, harbouring or receipt of persons, by means of the threat or the use of force or other forms of coercion, or abduction, of fraud, of deception, of the abuse of power or of the position of vulnerability or of the receiving of benefits to achieve the consent of a person having control over another person, for the exploitation. Exploitation shall include, at a minimum, the exploitation of the prostitution of others or other forms of sexual exploitation, forced labour or services, slavery or practices similar to slavery, servitude or the removal of organs.

(b) The consent of the victim of trafficking to the intended exploitation set forth in subparagraph (a) of this article shall be irrelevant where any of the means set forth in subparagraph (a) have been used.

(c) The recruitment, transportation, transfer, harbouring or receipt of a child for the purpose of exploitation shall be considered "human trafficking" even if this does not involve any of the means set forth in subparagraph (a) of this article.

(d) 'Child' shall mean any person less than eighteen years of age.

Source: A/RES/55/25, UN Trafficking Protocol, Annex II

A system of human rights monitoring mechanisms in the form of 'treaty-monitoring bodies' has been set up under various conventions to help UN member states to assess their performance in discharging their human rights obligations. However, as Janie Chuang points out, 'unlike human rights treaties, the Trafficking Protocol does not establish a treaty-monitoring body with powers to resolve the interpretative disputes or to assess individual state compliance with protocol obligations' (2014: 616). Instead, the Protocol relies on the UNODC to provide 'technical and legislative guidance and to oversee research and analysis in the area of human trafficking (Chuang 2014: 616–617).

The CoE Convention was opened for signature in 2005. It extends the definition of human trafficking, stipulating that human trafficking may or may not be linked with organised crime (2005). All CoE members have ratified the Convention. In 2013, Belarus became the first non-CoE state to ratify the Convention. Despite this high incidence of accession, implementation of the CoE Convention's provisions has been inconsistent.

Human trafficking is explicitly prohibited by the Charter of Fundamental Rights of the European Union, and the EU has made combating human trafficking a priority of its programmes in the fields of justice and home affairs. In 2002, the EU Council adopted a Framework Decision on combating human trafficking which served as basis for the development of a comprehensive approach across the member states. In the context of the Stockholm Programme, Framework Decision 2002/629/JHA was replaced with Directive 2011/36/EC, known as the Trafficking Directive, which today defines the minimum common rules for identifying offences of human trafficking within the EU. The Trafficking Directive adopts a wide definition of human trafficking by including other forms of exploitation comprising prostitution or other forms of sexual exploitation, forced labour or services, practices similar to slavery or servitude and begging.

For Ronald Weitzer, 'definitional problems plague both scholarly and policy discussions of human trafficking' (2014: 7). In particular, a lack of consensus between national jurisdictions as to the boundary, if any, between trafficking in human beings and people smuggling complicates efforts in international law to distinguish between these crimes. Moreover, the way in which the definition of human trafficking is expressed in the

Trafficking Protocol has also been subject to criticism for its opacity, ambiguity and complexity, with its critics contending that it lacks clarity of meaning or legal interpretation and avoids common definitions of recruitment, deception, coercion or exploitation (Gallagher 2015). This has influenced the effectiveness of the law enforcement response to trafficking in states that have adopted the definitional clauses of the Trafficking Protocol verbatim in their own national legislation. Mike Dottridge argues that, given the complexity of the Trafficking Protocol's definition, 'in most contexts it does not function well as an operational definition for law enforcement agencies or others, such as immigration officials [who] consequently resort to various shortcuts to enforce the law and, in doing so, often misapply or misinterpret the definition' (2007: 4). Moreover, in some states that have adopted the precise wording of the Trafficking Protocol's definition in their national legislation without further context, a narrow legal interpretation has been applied, restricting human trafficking to a transnational context. Other states have maintained a clear distinction between legislation prohibiting human trafficking and alternative legislation addressing specific forms of exploitation mentioned in the Trafficking Protocol, resulting in victims of internal trafficking not being recognised and, hence, not being provided with the protection or assistance envisaged by the Trafficking Protocol or by other international instruments (ICAT 2012).

Whilst the Trafficking Protocol is a criminal protocol and was never intended to be a human rights instrument, its drafters did explicitly intend to encourage international cooperation in fighting human trafficking as a crime. Thus, it in no way detracts from applicable human rights law. Arguably, the original definition of human trafficking was not fit for purpose. There are no common definitions of recruitment, deception or coercion, and exploitation is not defined, but rather described, allowing states to elaborate forms of exploitation when defining human trafficking in national legislation. Trafficking has also been conceptualised within the framework of transnational organised crime. Article 5 of UNTOC refers to the criminalisation of participation in an organised criminal group and Article 2 defines an 'organised criminal group' as a 'structured group of three or more persons, existing for a period of time and acting in concert with the aim of committing one or more serious crimes or offences'. These definitions appear to preclude the commission of human trafficking offences by individual traffickers or criminal networks that are either randomly formed or not structured.

The obligation under Article 5 of the Trafficking Protocol for States Parties to establish a criminal offence of human trafficking in their own legal systems is directly linked to the definition of human trafficking set out in Article 3, and it is this definition which is, therefore, central to any legislation seeking to implement the Trafficking Protocol (UNODC 2004b). This definition (see Box 1.1) consists of a combination of three elements, each of which must be taken from a list set out in the definition. The definition states that to qualify as a violation of the article, each of these three elements must be present. These component elements fall into the categories of 'action'; 'means' and 'purpose'. Action includes the recruitment, transportation, transfer, harbouring or receipt of persons. Means includes the threat or use of force or other forms of coercion, of abduction, of fraud, of deception, of the abuse of power or of a position of vulnerability or of giving or receiving of payments or benefits to a person in control of the victim. Purpose includes, at a minimum, the exploitation or prostitution of others or other forms of sexual exploitation, forced labour or services, slavery or practices similar to slavery, servitude and the removal of organs.

Whilst the Trafficking Protocol seemingly defines human trafficking as a simple crime comprising three components, when studied more closely, human trafficking often involves a complex *process* involving multiple actors. The first component of the definition, the 'action' element, is one part, and in the case of trafficking in children, the only part, of the definition that constitutes an explicit criminal element of the crime of human trafficking. This element can be fulfilled by a variety of activities including, but not limited to, the practices of recruitment, transportation, transferring, harbouring or receipt of persons, the specifics of which are not defined in the Trafficking Protocol.

The final element of the definition, 'for the purpose of exploitation' introduces a requirement of 'wrongful intention' into the definition.

Trafficking will occur if the implicated individual or entity intended that the action (which in the case of trafficking in adults must have occurred or been made possible through one of the stipulated means) would lead to exploitation. Trafficking is, thereby, a crime of specific or special intent. (UNODC 2014b)

In international law the offence of human trafficking is completed once a trafficker recruits a potential victim with the intention to exploit. Exploitation can take place either across a border or within the borders of a state, and the recruitment can also take place either outside or within the borders of a state. Consequently, the offence of human trafficking as defined in Article 3 of the Trafficking Protocol is completed at a very early stage. No exploitation needs to have taken place for the offence of human trafficking to have occurred.

The obligation under the Trafficking Protocol is to criminalise human trafficking as a combination of constituent elements rather than criminalising the elements themselves. Thus, 'any conduct that combines any listed action and means and is carried out for any of the listed purposes must be criminalised as trafficking' (UNODC 2004a). The *crime* of human trafficking can be a continuing offence, take place over a period of time and involve multiple actors. The *elements* of human trafficking can be either concurrent with one another or can overlap. An important aspect of the definition is an understanding of human trafficking as interrelated actions rather than a single act at a given point in time. Once initial control of a victim is secured, she/he is, commonly, moved to a place where there is a market for her/his services which can be a place where the victim does not understand the language and is unable to seek help. This activity can take place within a state's territorial borders or across borders, with recruitment taking place in one state and the reception and exploitation of the victim taking place in another. Whether or not an international border is crossed, the intention to exploit the individual concerned underpins the entire process.

The purpose of human trafficking is the exploitation of the victim and, hence, exploitation is an essential element of the trafficking offence. The act of human trafficking is constituted before any exploitation occurs, as it is the trafficker's purpose or intent to exploit, not the actual exploitation that completes the third element of the crime of trafficking. Exploitation is not defined in the Trafficking Protocol, and the onus is on each country to provide a definition. As accepted by the UNODC, 'exploitation is not well or uniformly understood' and 'certain forms of exploitation raise particular practical and evidentiary challenges' (2015: 11). This can result in problems in defining exploitation and incorporating it into national legislation. It can also make it difficult to identify victims in exploitative situations and recognise different forms of exploitation, especially since new forms of exploitation are still being conceived and discovered. If all the elements of human trafficking are present, including exploitation or the intent to exploit, then the offence of human trafficking can be established and the victims of trafficking can be identified.

The means are the methods used by the perpetrators to recruit potential victims. The means listed in the Trafficking Protocol have been accepted as a distinct and important part of the international legal definition of human trafficking and include abduction, fraud, deception, coercion and the abuse of a position of vulnerability (APOV).

Abduction is the act of forcibly seizing someone against their will and can include forcibly taking a child from his or her parent. There is no specific definition of abduction in relation to human trafficking. In the context of human trafficking, the definition of fraud includes acts of deception which mislead a person by words or conduct about the nature of work or services to be provided, for example, promises of legitimate work, the conditions of work, the extent to which the person will be free to leave her or his place of residence or other circumstances involving exploitation of the person constitute abduction (OSCE 2011).

The definition of fraud includes acts of deception understood as misleading a person by words or conduct about the nature of work or services to be provided such as misrepresenting the conditions of employment or the extent to which the person will be free to leave her/his place of residence or other circumstances involving exploitation of the person. Deception can include giving false or inaccurate or misleading information such as when recruiting employing workers into forced labour or the offer of false job for sexual exploitation.

Coercion is an umbrella term for a range of behaviours including violence, threats, deceit and APOV. In the Trafficking Protocol, it is linked to, but is not synonymous with, the threat or use of force which can be either against the victim or a member of her/his family. More problematic has been the definition of psychological coercion. For example, threats aimed at provoking the disapproval or rejection of a victim from a family or peer group, or inciting anger or displeasure towards a victim from a person considered to be a partner or boy/girlfriend or other forms of blackmail may constitute psychological coercion.

Definitional ambiguities can, however, make it easier for the trafficker to conceal psychological coercion (Hopper and Hidalgo 2006). The nexus between physical and psychological coercion produces a particularly virulent method of exerting control over victims. Yet, whilst there are examples of national courts being willing to stretch the definition of coercion beyond physical violence or the threat of violence, there are warnings that these less direct forms of coercion can cause difficulties for courts. For example, Pakistan's Sindh High Court rejected the argument that this type of indirect threat might constitute coercion, asking the rhetorical question 'can a worker be bound by "mental detention" instead of "physical walls and chains"' (ILO 2009: 5).

Economic coercion involves victims being forced to pay excessive amounts of money, having significant salary deductions or not being paid at all. A common form of economic coercion is debt bondage referring to a system which keeps victims working to pay off actual or imagined debts (OSCE 2011). Benjamin Buckland defines debt bondage as a

> status or condition arising from a pledge by a debtor of his personal services or those of a person under his control as a security for a debt, if the value of those services as reasonably assessed is not applied towards the liquidation of the debt or the length and nature of those services are not respectively limited or defined. (2009: 146)

As debt bondage cases often do not involve violence or deprivation of freedom of movement, but rather non-payment or under-paying of salaries, the gravity of these crimes is not consistently recognised.

The concept of APOV, together with the other means listed in the Trafficking Protocol, is a distinct and important part of the international legal definition of human trafficking. It has survived intact in all major treaties adopted after the Trafficking Protocol that incorporate a definition of human trafficking, as well as in policy documents and interpretative texts (UNODC 2013). There is no explicit definition in the Trafficking Protocol of 'vulnerability' in relation to human trafficking, but there are defined causes or factors that can make a person vulnerable to being exploited as a victim of human trafficking or susceptible to being re-trafficked. Vulnerability can be a critical indicator when identifying victims and an accurate assessment of vulnerability can help to ensure that victim and/or witnesses are appropriately supported and protected. APOV is any situation in which the person involved has no real acceptable alternative but to submit to the abuse involved. The drafting history of the Trafficking Protocol confirms that APOV refers to 'any situation in which the person involved has no real and acceptable alternative but to submit to the abuse involved' (UNODC 2013: 6).

The UNODC states that APOV occurs when an individual's 'personal, situational or circumstantial vulnerability is intentionally used or otherwise taken advantage of, to recruit, transport, transfer, harbour or receive that person for the purpose of exploiting him or her, such that the person believes that submitting to the will of the abuser is the only real or acceptable option available to him or her, and that belief is reasonable in light of the victim's situation' (UNODC 2012: 2). The existence of vulnerability is assessed on a case-by-case basis. Situational vulnerability may relate to a person's legal status and/or their potential linguistic or ethnic marginalisation. Circumstantial vulnerability may relate to a person's lack of income or homelessness. Such vulnerabilities can be pre-existing or can be created by the trafficker (UNODC 2013). In each case, 'it has to be established whether (1) there was a position of vulnerability, and, if so, (2) whether the suspect intentionally abused that position to secure the "act" element of the offence' (Esser and Dettmeijer-Vermeulen 2016).

In 2012, the UNODC reported a wide variation in the way in which this means, notably the interpretation of a 'position of vulnerability', is understood (UNODC 2012). In the UK, APOV has become a controversial potential defence for offenders involved in the related criminal activities of 'county lines', 'commuting' and 'cuckooing'. These criminal phenomena involve city-based drug dealers extending their reach into coastal and rural markets, often using 'vulnerable' young drug addicts to transport and sell the drugs. The UK criminal justice system faces the dilemma of countering drug trafficking in these new markets, whilst protecting the vulnerable young people coerced into working in the drug trade. However, although they may well be vulnerable, the young people involved in this criminal activity are equally aware that APOV, as well as the CoE Convention's non-punishment provision (see Chap. 4), potentially offers them a ready-made defence against the crime of drug trafficking. Acknowledging that 'we cannot simply arrest our way out of this problem', Leah Moyle, citing Katie Ellis, nonetheless, recognises that 'the notion of vulnerability may contradict life experiences in which involvement in criminality or exploitative labour may otherwise be understood as demonstrating a certain level of autonomy' (Moyle 2019: 14; Ellis 2018).

Perpetrators of trafficking earn profits from their victims through differing exploitative forms of human trafficking. However, in order to sustain their profit, they must ensure that victims remain within exploitative conditions. This is achieved through different, often violent mechanisms that may be used in isolation, but often are used concurrently to create the conditions of actual or psychological imprisonment. Control methods include isolation, removal of documents and/or use or the threat of violence.

Isolation can be used deliberately to control victims to ensure that they do not escape from the trafficking situation. Language acts as a barrier as victims often do not speak the language of the country into which they have been trafficked and the trafficker ensures they are given no opportunity to learn. Victims can be moved from location to location so they are unable to make any ties, and they may be denied access to a telephone or other communication devices. These methods of isolation are designed to make the victim more reliant on the traffickers.

> Human traffickers systematically isolate their victims, creating a sense of disconnection from others. Traffickers utilise verbal abuse and humiliation to impact their victims' sense of self. They create an environment of fear

through threats of harm to victims or their families. This chronic fear acti-
vation can lead to psychological changes that impair the ability of victims
to mobilise the physical and psychological resources needed by the victim
to escape. Their natural survival mechanisms break down, and their own
bodies betray them. This physical and psychological erosion becomes the
tie that binds victims into slavery. (Hopper and Hidalgo 2006: 185)

The confiscation or removal of the victim's documents by the traffickers
can make it almost impossible for them to leave the trafficking situation.
This is usually done when the victim arrives at the destination and without documents they have no official identity which limits the possibility
of escape.

The use or threat of violence is also used to control victims, especially
to ensure that they do not escape from the trafficking situation. Violence
may also be used against a victim to intimidate other victims. Violence or
the threat of violence to members of the victim's family is particularly
effective, especially when the victim either knows or believes that the trafficker knows the whereabouts of her/his family.

The three-part definition of human trafficking derived from the
Trafficking Protocol forms the basis of guidance disseminated by core
intergovernmental organisations such as the UNODC and the
Organization for Security and Cooperation in Europe (OSCE), the
world's largest security-oriented intergovernmental organisation. This
training documentation is intended to define the boundaries of the crime
of human trafficking in international law and encourage a uniform
understanding of what constitutes human trafficking. The Protocol is
intended to create 'consistency and consensus around the world' as to the
nature of the crime of human trafficking, and Article 5 of the Protocol
requires States Parties to criminalise human trafficking in 'accordance
with domestic legal systems'. The *travaux préparatoires*, the official record
of the negotiations that led to the Trafficking Protocol, indicate that at an
early stage of drafting 'human trafficking' was taken to refer to a process
denoting connectivity between the individual elements. Yet, the actual
extent to which the requirement for the three elements to operate together
in order to secure a prosecution in individual domestic jurisdictions is
debatable. There is evidence that, rather than emphasising process, the

constituent elements of human trafficking have been treated as distinct, enabling a criminal offence to be proved without necessarily establishing each individual element. As Chuang comments,

> recollections of those present during the negotiations confirm that the structure of the act element was assumed to reflect the drafters' vision of trafficking as a process that multiple actors carried out in concert. States separated out each act in the process in order to criminalize all the actors involved—the recruiters, transporters, owners, and supervisors of any place of exploitation—rather than to equate the individual components of that process with their sum. (2014: 631)

The way in which the offence of human trafficking has been defined in domestic legislation may avoid the process approach evidently envisaged in the Trafficking Protocol. For example, Argentina's 'Law on the Prevention and Sanctioning of Human Trafficking and Assistance to Victims' as amended only requires the act and purpose elements of the Tracking Protocol with the coercive means element only relevant in a prosecution as aggravating circumstances. Legislation adopted by States Parties to comply with the requirements of the Trafficking Protocol varies considerably (UNODC n.d.; EU Commission n.d.). Chuang argues that 'collapsing' the three-part definition renders the offence of human trafficking the equivalent of 'exploitation', the last of the three elements, since the act and means elements would typically be satisfied by the inherently coercive nature of the end result—for example, exploitation in the form of forced labour or slavery-like practices (2014: 632). Yet, in her submission to the Joint Committee on the UK's Draft Modern Slavery Bill, Anne Gallagher advised that the offence of 'trafficking in persons' should be retained since

> some cases will be suitable for this charge. Particularly egregious or large-scale cases may benefit from the relatively greater attention and expertise that is often available for 'trafficking cases'. In addition, as an internationally recognised concept, 'trafficking' provides a solid basis for collaboration and cooperation (including international legal cooperation) between countries. (Gallagher 2014)

However, Gallagher also recommended supplementing the offence of 'trafficking in persons' with other separate offences that reflect 'forms of exploitation that are associated with trafficking but for the purposes of criminal law do not require proof of "act" and "means"' (2014). For Gallagher, this approach would provide more flexibility to prosecutors,

> and also allows a national criminal justice system to ensure the complexities of establishing the three separate elements of 'trafficking' do not act as a barrier to prosecuting exploitation. Related offences should be linked to the umbrella offence of trafficking (or another means should be used) to ensure that provisions applicable under 'trafficking' (most particularly concerning victim protection and support) are applicable to those offences. (2014)

Those states that are members of the Council of Europe are presumed not to act in such a way as to contravene the European Convention on Human Rights (ECHR). Article 4 of the ECHR prohibits slavery, servitude and forced labour. The ECHR is supervised by the European Court of Human Rights (ECtHR), and several decisions of the Court have had an impact on a state's obligations to victims of trafficking. National courts also have an obligation to apply the ECHR and judgments against states, for violations of the ECHR are binding on the states concerned and they are obliged to execute them. National courts must also take into account any judgment, decision or declaration or advisory opinion of the ECtHR when determining any question that arises in relation to Article 4 of the ECHR. This is because Article 4 prohibits slavery, servitude and forced or compulsory labour, and whilst the criminal offence of human trafficking is defined in national law, it is also defined in part by reference to Article 4 (Drew 2009). Moreover, there is no derogation permitted in respect of the prohibition on slavery and servitude.

Cases in which Article 4 has been germane include *Van der Mussele v Belgium* in which the ECtHR ruled on the definition of 'forced labour' under ILO Convention No.29 concerning 'Forced or Compulsory Labour', which defined forced labour as 'all work or service that is exacted from any person under the menace of any penalty and for which the said person has not offered himself voluntarily'. The Court held that this definition was a starting point for the interpretation of Article 4 of the

ECHR. Notwithstanding actual consent, forced or compulsory labour may exist where a considerable and unreasonable imbalance exists between obligations undertaken by the worker and the specific aim of that labour. This definition echoes the definition of debt bondage, and courts should be willing to look beyond actual subjective consent to the objective terms and conditions of work (Drew 2009).

Siliadin v France was the first judgment the ECtHR considered under the CoE Convention in the context of Article 4 of the ECHR. The Court concluded that the applicant, a minor at the time, had been subjected to forced labour and was held in servitude within the meaning of Article 4 of the CoE Convention. The Court unequivocally stated that, 'it necessarily follows from this provision [Article 4] that States have positive obligations, in the same way as under Article 3 for example, to adopt criminal law provisions which penalise the practices referred to in Article 4 and to apply them in practice'.

Rantsev v Cyprus and Russia (see Box 1.2) is an important case where the ECtHR found that human trafficking, although not explicitly

---

Box 1.2   Case of Rantsev vs. Cyprus and Russia

Rantsev v Cyprus and Russia, Application no. 25965/04

A Russian national, Ms Rantseva, entered Cyprus on an artiste visa (often used by traffickers to bring women into a country for purposes of forced prostitution). She escaped from the club where she was working, but her employers/traffickers found her and brought her to a police station in order to have her deported for violating the terms of her visa. The police decided not to pursue deportation and called her employers/traffickers to collect her. She was later found dead outside the house of one of her employers/traffickers.

The applicant, Ms Rantseva's father, complained that the Cypriot authorities had failed to investigate allegations of human trafficking and protecting his daughter.

The European Court of Human Rights found that Article 4 of the ECHR had been violated. The Court clarified that States parties have a positive obligation to investigate allegations of trafficking and to implement measures to prevent and protect people from human trafficking.

Source: European Court of Human Rights. Available at https://ec.europa.eu/anti-trafficking/sites/antitrafficking/files/rantsev_vs_russia_cyprus_en_4.pdf

mentioned in the ECHR, falls within the scope of Article 4 of the ECHR which prohibits slavery, servitude and forced labour. The Court took a much more thorough look at the issue of human trafficking, clarifying the obligations of states to have in place adequate protection measures for victims of trafficking and for potential victims.

Human Trafficking and Modern Slavery

The 1970s saw the emergence in UN and NGO circles of the term 'modern slavery' to reflect the notion that contemporary forms of labour and sexual exploitation ostensibly resembled historical manifestations of slavery, although the term and concept did not gain traction at the time. Following the adoption of the Trafficking Protocol in 2000, however, the term entered into wider usage, and closer attention was paid to the corollary of this shift in terminology. Kevin Bales was an early and vocal advocate of modern slavery as the most accurate term and concept to encapsulate prevalent forms of labour and sexual exploitation.

> A common question is why these practices should be called slavery rather than just another form of super-exploitation. The answer is simple. Throughout history, slavery has meant a loss of free will and choice backed up by violence, sometimes exercised by the slaveholder, sometimes by elements of the state…Granted workers at the bottom of the economic ladder have few options to begin with, but at some point on the continuum of exploitation, even those options are lost. These workers are unable to walk away. (Bales 2002)

That slavery is not an artefact of history but a reality of modern life attracted the interest of philanthropists, politicians and NGOs. In 2011, the WFF was established and, in 2013, the first edition of the Global Slavery Index was published. In 2014, a Global Fund to End Modern Slavery was proposed and, by 2017, it was receiving considerable funding from business and governments including the US and UK governments.

However, as the concept of modern slavery has become more mainstream, it has also become the target of criticism. Dottridge argues that the Western-centric interpretation of modern slavery, and its vigorous promotion as a new paradigm by states such as the UK and the US, is potentially neocolonial and culturally domineering (2017). Indeed, by labelling all exploitative practices as a form of 'slavery', advocates of modern slavery hinder efforts to mitigate traditional forms of exploitation, such as bonded labour, which fall short of chattel slavery (Dottridge 2017).

Two states in the forefront of the adoption of the wider concept of modern slavery are the UK and Australia. With the entry into law of the Modern Slavery Act (2015), the UK became the first jurisdiction since the adoption of the Trafficking Protocol to seek to counter the crime of modern slavery rather than human trafficking. The Modern Slavery Act

> repeals and replaces offences of human trafficking arising under section 59A Sexual Offences Act 2003 (inserted by section 109 of the Protection of Freedoms Act 2012) and section 4 Asylum and Immigration (Treatment of Claimants) Act 2004. The Act also repeals and replaces the offence of holding another person in slavery or servitude or requiring another person to perform forced or compulsory labour arising under section 71 Coroners and Justice Act 2009. (CPS 2019)

Rose Broad and Nick Turnbull argue that the Modern Slavery Act itself 'played a crucial role in constructing slavery as a problem, as much as it aimed to solve it' (2019: 132). Their analysis of the context in which the Act was proposed identifies a political dimension to its drafting that reflects the anti-immigration policies of the sitting Conservative government in the strategic shift from countering human trafficking to targeting modern slavery. For Broad and Turnbull, 'this top-down process, along with the strong moral component of global anti-slavery discourse, encouraged a law enforcement response, excluding engagement with the marginalised populations the law was designed to assist' (2019: 132). The framing of the legislation consciously privileged a criminal justice approach to tackling forms of exploitation, rather than addressing the fundamental causes of exploitation or the treatment of those being exploited. This chimes with Dottridge's assessment of the Modern Slavery Act.

> The use of the term 'modern slavery' has potentially damaging consequences for the very people whom [the] new law is supposed to protect. The prime problem is that the term implies a degree of exploitation that is

so extreme as to fall outside the ordinary world of work. It also implies that such exploitation cannot be solved by any of the techniques that have been traditionally used to combat work place abuse, such as regulation, work place inspections and the formation by workers of associations to defend themselves against abuse, and trade unions. (Dottridge 2017)

Likewise, Virginia Mantouvalou argues that the Modern Slavery Act 'has not been successful in meeting the key aim of increasing prosecutions, and has not provided adequate civil remedies to victims' (2018: 1045). The Act's privileging of a criminalisation approach also 'obscures the role of the law as a structure that creates relations of subordination' (Mantouvalou 2018: 1045). For legislation to be effective it needs to balance criminalisation with effective protection of workers' rights and civil remedies where rights have not been upheld. For Mantouvalou there is 'little evidence of such effective protection of workers' rights in the Modern Slavery Act or the broader legislative framework' (2018: 1045).

The term 'slavery' is defined by the Convention to Suppress the Slave Trade and Slavery (1926) as 'the condition of a person over whom any or all of the powers attaching to the right of ownership are exercised'. This expression of chattel slavery was expanded by the Supplementary Convention to the Abolition of Slavery, the Slave Trade and Institutions and Practices Similar to Slavery (1956) to also apply to 'slavery-like practices, including debt bondage, serfdom, servile forms of marriage and exploitation of children'. The term 'modern slavery' is, however, not defined in international law. In February 2017, an inquiry was established to report on establishing a Modern Slavery Act in Australia. In its submission to the inquiry, the UNODC expressed concern over the growing use of the term modern slavery.

While 'modern day slavery' might be useful as an advocacy and umbrella term that seeks to bring together the variety of situations in which a person is forcibly or subtly controlled by an individual or a group for the purpose of exploitation, UNODC notes that there is no internationally agreed definition of 'modern day slavery' or 'modern slavery', let alone the legal definition of the term. (Parliament of the Commonwealth of Australia 2017: 30)

In her submission to the inquiry, Gallagher pointed out that the 'concepts that are typically subsumed under its umbrella, namely: slavery; servitude; trafficking in persons; forced labour; debt bondage; forced marriage; and sale of or sexual exploitation of children...are defined in international legal instruments to which most states, including Australia, are party' (Parliament of the Commonwealth of Australia 2017: 30). This position was supported by Nicole Sillars who argued that 'from a substantive criminal law perspective, the [Australian] Criminal Code is also far more detailed and instructive than the UK Modern Slavery Act...the introduction of the term 'modern slavery' into Australian criminal law is therefore redundant and unnecessary' (Parliament of the Commonwealth of Australia 2017: 42).

For Chuang, the trend towards incorporating previously separate exploitative offences under the umbrella of modern slavery could lead to the effective demise of trafficking as an offence: 'doctrinal grounds for conflating forced labour, trafficking, and slavery are shaky at best and could prove to be quicksand for the very idea of trafficking as a freestanding legal concept' (2014: 629).

Conclusion

Human trafficking constitutes one of the most serious threats facing global society in the early twenty-first century. There are concerns over the Global Slavery Index using the broader concept of modern slavery not recognised in international law, rather than the narrower concept of human trafficking which is the focus of this book. Nonetheless, the Index's high and rising estimates of the numbers being trafficked for labour, sex and other purposes are, for the most part, substantiated by evidence collected by national and international agencies. At the same time, the data available suggests that, globally, the number of prosecutions and convictions remain static.

Countering the threat of human trafficking is challenging. A fundamental obstacle for law enforcement and criminal justice agencies is determining whether a particular instance of exploitation constitutes the crime of trafficking. The definition of human trafficking in the Protocol is not straightforward. The three elements required to prove the crime—action, means and purpose—are not explicitly defined and require definition and clarification by individual domestic legislation and case law. In the absence of a treaty body for the Trafficking Protocol, the UNODC, alongside other international organisations such as the OSCE, has sought, with only partial success, to develop a common global understanding and application of the law as it applies to human trafficking. Lack of definitional clarity has led to individual jurisdictions adopting discrete interpretations of key concepts, for example, the meaning of vulnerability, with a consequent impact on the identification of trafficked victims.

The distinctive legal construction of the crime developed by the Trafficking Protocol sought to frame human trafficking as a process involving three constituent elements. A universal acknowledgement of this objective has proved difficult to achieve both in terms of legislation and the practice of law enforcement agencies at domestic level. Whilst supra-national mechanisms, notably the Trafficking Directive, and an overarching counter-trafficking strategy mean that EU member states should share a common understanding of the crime of human trafficking, in practice there remain differences in criminal justice and law enforcement approaches. The clearest example of this divergence is the decision by the UK to move its focus from individual crimes of exploitation such as human trafficking to the umbrella crime of modern slavery. With other jurisdictions such as Australia, and potentially the US, following the UK's lead, further dilution of human trafficking as a standalone offence remains a possibility.

References

Aronowitz, A. (2017), *Human Trafficking*. Santa Barbara: ABC-CLIO.
Association of South-East Asian Nations (2010), *ASEAN Handbook on International Legal Cooperation in Trafficking in Persons Cases*. Jakarta: ASEAN.
Bales, K. (2002), 'The Social Psychology of Modern Slavery', Scientific American, April. Available at https://www.scientificamerican.com/article/the-social-psychology-of/.

Bosco F., Di Cortemiglia, V., and Serojitdinov, A. (2009), 'Human Trafficking Patterns' in Friesendorf, C. (ed.), *Strategies Against Human Trafficking: The Role of the Security Sector*, Vienna and Geneva: National Defence Academy and Austrian Ministry of Defence and Sports.

Broad, R., and Turnbull, N. (2019), 'From Human Trafficking to Modern Slavery: The Development of Anti-Trafficking Policy in the UK', *European Journal on Criminal Policy and Research*, Vol. 25.

Buckland, B. (2009). 'Human Trafficking and Smuggling: Crossover and Overlap', in Friesendorf, C. (ed.), *Strategies Against Human Trafficking: The Role of the Security Sector*, Vienna and Geneva: National Defence Academy and Austrian Ministry of Defence and Sports.

Chuang, J. (2014), 'Exploitation Creep and the Unmaking of Human Trafficking Law, *American Journal of International Law*, Vol. 108, No. 4.

Crown Prosecution Service (2019), 'Human Trafficking, Smuggling and Slavery', *Legal Guidance International and Organised Crime*, September 2019. Available at https://www.cps.gov.uk/legal-guidance/human-trafficking-smuggling-and-slavery.

Danziger R., Martens J., and Guajardo M., (2009), 'Human Trafficking & Migration Management' in Friesendorf, C. (ed.), Strategies Against Human Trafficking: The Role of the Security Sector, Vienna and Geneva: National Defence Academy and Austrian Ministry of Defence and Sports.

De Vries, I, Nickerson, C., Farrell, A., Wittmer-Wolfe, D., and Bouché, V. (2019), 'Anti-immigration sentiment and public opinion on human trafficking', *Crime, Law and Social Change*, Vol. 72, No. 1.

Dottridge, M. (2007), *Collateral Damage: The Impact of Anti-Trafficking Measures on Human Rights around the World*. Bangkok: Global Alliance Against Traffic in Women.

Dottridge, M. (2017), 'Eight reasons why we shouldn't use the term "modern slavery"', Open Democracy, October. Available at https://www.opendemocracy.net/en/beyond-trafficking-and-slavery/eight-reasons-why-we-shouldnt-use-term-modern-slavery/.

Drew, S. (2009), *Human Trafficking-Human Rights*. London: Legal Action Group.

Dwyer, P., Lewis, H., Scullion, L., and Waite, L. (2011), 'Forced labour and UK immigration policy: status matters?' Joseph Rowntree Foundation programme paper, 13th October. Available at https://www.jrf.org.uk/report/forced-labour-and-uk-immigration-policy-status-matters.

Ellis, K. (2018), 'Contested vulnerability: A case study of girls in secure care', *Children and Youth Services Review*, No. 88.

Esser, L., and Dettmeijer-Vermeulen, C. (2016), 'The Prominent Role of National Judges in Interpreting the International Definition of Human Trafficking', *Anti-Trafficking Review*, No. 6.

European Commission (2012), 'The EU Strategy towards the Eradication of Trafficking in Human Beings 2012–2016', June. Available at https://ec.europa.eu/anti-trafficking/sites/antitrafficking/files/eu_strategy_towards_the_eradication_of_trafficking_in_human_beings_2012-2016_1.pdf.

European Commission (n.d.), 'Together Against Human Trafficking'. Available at https://ec.europa.eu/anti-trafficking/member-states_en.

Eurostat (2015), *Trafficking in Human Beings*. Luxemburg: Publications Office of the European Union.

Eurostat (2018), *Data Collection on the Trafficking in Human Beings*. Luxemburg: Publications Office of the European Union.

Gallagher, A. (2001), 'Human Rights and the New UN Protocols on Trafficking and Migrant Smuggling: A Preliminary Analysis', *Human Rights Quarterly*, Vol. 23, No. 4.

Gallagher, A. (2014), 'Submission to the Joint Committee on the Draft Modern Slavery Bill', March. Available at http://data.parliament.uk/writtenevidence/committeeevidence.svc/evidencedocument/draft-modern-slavery-bill-committee/draft-modern-slavery-bill/written/7406.pdf.

Gallagher, A (2015), 'Two Cheers for the Trafficking Protocol', *Anti-Trafficking Review*, Issue 4.

Global Slavery Index (2018), 'Modern Slavery: A Hidden, Everyday Problem'. Available at https://www.globalslaveryindex.org/.

Guardian (2017), 'Using security as Brexit bargaining chip is reckless and lacks credibility'. Available at https://www.theguardian.com/politics/2017/mar/30/using-security-as-brexit-bargaining-chip-is-reckless-and-lacks-credibility.

Haynes, D. (2007), '(Not) Found Chained to a Bed in a Brothel: Conceptual, Legal, and Procedural Failures to Fulfill the Promise of the Trafficking Victims Protection Act', *Georgetown Immigration Law Journal*, Vol. 21, No. 3.

Hopper, E., and Hidalgo, J. (2006), 'Invisible chains: Psychological coercion of human trafficking victims', *Intercultural Human Rights Law Review*, Vol. 1.

Inter-Agency Coordination Group against Trafficking in Persons (2012), *The International Legal Frameworks concerning Trafficking in Persons*. Vienna: ICAT

Inter-Agency Coordination Group against Trafficking in Persons (2014), *Preventing Trafficking in Persons by Addressing Demand*. Vienna: ICAT

International Labour Organisation (2009), *Forced Labour and Human Trafficking: Casebook of Court Decisions*. Geneva: ILO.

International Labour Organisation (ILO) and Walk Free Foundation (2017), *Global estimates of modern slavery: forced labour and forced marriage*. Geneva: ILO and Walk Free Foundation.

Mantouvalou, V. (2018), 'The UK Modern Slavery Act 2015 Three Years On', *Modern Law Review*, Vol. 88, No. 6.

Massari, M. (2015), 'At the Edge of Europe: the phenomenon of Irregular Migration from Libya to Italy' in Massey, S. and Coluccello, S. (eds), *Eurafrican Migration: Legal, Economic and Social responses to Irregular Migration*. Basingstoke: Palgrave Pivot.

Mo, C. (2018), 'Perceived Relative Deprivation and Risk: An Aspiration-Based Model of Human Trafficking Vulnerability', *Political Behavior*, Vol. 40, No. 1.

Moyle, L. (2019), 'Situating Vulnerability and Exploitation in Street-Level Drug Markets: Cuckooing, Commuting, and the "County Lines" Drug Supply Model', *Journal of Drug Issues*, Vol. 49, No. 4.

National Crime Agency (2019), 'National referral mechanism statistics – end of year summary 2018', 20th March. Available at https://www.nationalcrime-agency.gov.uk/who-we-are/publications/282-national-referral-mechanism-sta-tistics-end-of-year-summary-2018/EOY18-MSHT%20NRM%20Annual%20Report%202018%20v1.0%20(1).pdf

Organization for Security and Cooperation in Europe (2011), 'Trafficking in Human Beings: Identification of Potential and Presumed Victims: a community policing approach', *SPMU Publication Series*, Vol. 12

Parliament of the Commonwealth of Australia (2017), *Hidden in Plain Sight: An inquiry into establishing a Modern Slavery Act in Australia*. Canberra: Commonwealth of Australia. Available at https://parlinfo.aph.gov.au/parlInfo/download/committees/reportjnt/024102/toc_pdf/HiddeninPlainSight.pdf;fileType=application%2Fpdf.

Salt, J., and Stein, J. (1997), 'Migration as a Business: The Case of Trafficking', *International Migration*, Vol. 35, No. 4.

Shelley, L. (2007), 'The rise and diversification of human smuggling and trafficking into the United States' in Thachuk, K. (ed.), *Transnational threats: Smuggling and trafficking in arms, drugs and human life*. Westport: Greenwood Publishing Group.

United Nations Office on Drugs and Crime (2013), 'Abuse of a position of vulnerability and other "means" within the definition of trafficking in persons', Issue Paper, April.

United Nations Office on Drugs and Crime (2018), *Global Report on Trafficking in Persons*. Vienna: UNODC.

United Nations Office on Drugs and Crime (2012), 'Guidance Note on 'abuse of a position of vulnerability' as a means of trafficking in persons in Article 3 of the Protocol to Prevent, Suppress and Punish Trafficking in Persons, Especially Women and Children, supplementing the United Nations Convention against Transnational Organised Crime'. Available at https://www.unodc.org/documents/human-trafficking/2012/UNODC_2012_Guidance_Note_-_Abuse_of_a_Position_of_Vulnerability_E.pdf.

United Nations Office on Drugs and Crime (n.d.), 'Human Trafficking Knowledge Portal'. Available at https://sherloc.unodc.org/cld/en/v3/htms/index.html.

United Nations Office on Drugs and Crime (2004a), *Legislative Guides for the Implementation of the UNTOC and Trafficking Protocols Thereto*. Vienna: UNODC.

United Nations Office on Drugs and Crime (2004b), *UN Convention Against Transnational Crime and the Trafficking Protocols Thereto*. Vienna: UNODC.

United Nations Office on Drugs and Crime (2015), 'The Concept of 'Exploitation' in the Trafficking in Persons Trafficking Protocol', *UNODC Issue Paper*. Available at https://www.unodc.org/documents/congress/background-information/Human_Trafficking/UNODC_2015_Issuc_Paper_Exploitation.pdf.

USAID (2010), *Trafficking of Adult Men in the Europe and Eurasia Region*, June. Available at http://lastradainternational.org/lsidocs/Trafficking%20of%20Men%20Draft_final.pdf.

Vogel, D., (2015), 'The Concept of Demand in the Context of Trafficking in Human Beings: Using contributions from economics in search of clarification' *DemandAT Working Paper*, No. 3, December. Available at https://www.demandat.eu/sites/default/files/DemandAT_WP3_Vogel_Economics_for_Conceptual_Clarification_FINAL2.pdf.

Weitzer, R. (2014), 'New Directions in Research on Human Trafficking', *Annals of the American Academy of Political and Social Science*, Vol. 653, No. 6.

2

Agency, Consent and Exploitation

Abstract Human trafficking and people smuggling are sometimes, erroneously, treated as interchangeable. The chapter outlines the apparently clear-cut distinction between human trafficking and people smuggling in international law, stressing that the distinction is less conspicuous in real-life cases. Human trafficking is a complex crime, and practitioners need specialist training to differentiate between those being trafficked who should be managed as victims and those being smuggled who are, in law, engaged in a crime. Identification rests on interpreting the way in which the ambiguous notions of consent and agency have been exercised by the trafficked/smuggled individual. Accurate identification is further hindered by the imprecision of the concept of exploitation in the UN Trafficking Protocol leading to divergent interpretations in different jurisdictions.

Keywords: People smuggling • Identification • Consent • Agency • Exploitation

© The Author(s) 2020
S. Massey, G. Rankin, *Exploiting People for Profit*,
https://doi.org/10.1057/978-1-137-43413-5_2

The differences between human trafficking and people smuggling, as well as the interrelationship between them, are key to framing an effective response to both crimes. Whilst human trafficking and people smuggling are sometimes, erroneously, treated as interchangeable, the distinction is important. There are differences in law between human trafficking and people smuggling in terms of the transnational component, the financial considerations, the methods of transport and the relationship between the victim and the trafficker and/or smuggler. Key to this distinction is an evaluation of the legal and ethical standing of 'consent' to the process.

In particular, the immigration policy of states and supra-national entities, such as the EU, guides and is guided by the distinction between trafficking and smuggling. The chapter firstly interrogates the often imprecise boundary between these two crimes/concepts. It continues by investigating how this distinction plays out in reality, questioning the indicators used by states to categorise migrants as either smuggled or trafficked. Finally, the chapter focuses on the nature of exploitation as the principle purpose under the Trafficking Protocol, considering how ambiguities concerning definition inhibit the effective prosecution of trafficking cases.

The Smuggling of Migrants

The 'smuggling of migrants' (SOM) is the illegal movement of people across borders. According to Frank Laczko, smuggling on the two main routes, between Africa and Europe and between South America and the US, generates $6.75 billion a year (Ferrier and Kaminsky 2017). This is, nonetheless, a long way short of the profits generated annually by human trafficking, estimated by the ILO at $150 billion a year (ILO 2014: 13–15). The UNODC estimated that, in 2015, over a million people were smuggled into Europe by crossing the eastern, western and central Mediterranean (2018: 55). These numbers have since dropped significantly. In 2016, the UNODC estimated about 800,000 undocumented migrants entered the US (2018: 58). According to the IOM, between 2000 and 2014, at least 40,000 migrants died in transit (Brian and Laczko 2014: 11).

SOM is the facilitated crossing of borders illegally, or residing illegally in another country, with the aim of making financial or other material profit. The profile of people smugglers varies widely and can readily change. Smugglers can range from professional criminals and transnational organised crime groups to large and small networks. There are many smugglers who run legitimate businesses, such as travel agents, but are also involved in SOM. Migrants are often smuggled by organised criminal networks that exploit the lack of legal opportunities to migrate available to those seeking a better life outside their home country. Those who are smuggled enter into a contract and pay the agreed fee either before departure, upon arrival or in instalments. The debt may be paid by the person who has been smuggled or a member of her/his family or community. The victims usually have freedom of movement and are not controlled by their smugglers. They are transported covertly or by using false documents. The criminal activities of people smugglers undermine the capacity of states to safeguard their sovereignty and combat crime and corruption both within and across their borders. When authorities in the states of origin, transit and destination do not effectively cooperate in their efforts to prevent SOM, smugglers take advantage of weak law enforcement and/or criminal justice responses to forge new routes and new methods of transportation through which to commit their crimes.

The SOM Protocol seeks to promote international cooperation to target criminal smugglers and protect those they smuggle (UNODC 2012). The SOM comprises three elements: the procurement of illegal entry or the illegal residence of a person, financial or other material gain, and the crossing of a border into another state. Article 6 of the SOM Protocol requires the criminalisation of such conduct and requires States Parties to criminalise the conduct of those 'enabling a person to remain in a state where the person is not a legal resident or citizen without complying with requirements for legally remaining by illegal means' in order to obtain a financial or other material benefit. Distinctive elements of SOM are that it is transnational only, it is a consensual process and those smuggled willingly enter into contracts to pay off debt owed to the smugglers.

SOM is often conflated by the public, but also by governments, and law enforcement and criminal justice agencies with human trafficking. Christiana Gregoriou and Ilse Ras point out that male irregular migrants are generally presumed smuggled, thus presumed as having consented to their movement, whereas female irregular migrants are generally presumed trafficked, as not having consented to movement. As a result, the (male) smuggled migrant is criminalised, whilst the (female) trafficked migrant is assigned victim-status. (2018: 5)

The distinction in international law between the two crimes, however, is important when seeking to ascertain and protect victims. Whilst there is a continuing debate in the scholarly literature regarding the nexus between smuggling and trafficking, there is equally the danger that confusing the two crimes can lead to human trafficking being treated as an immigration issue, rather than a human rights issue that requires a policy response within and across governments. Human trafficking and SOM have similar push factors which can include relative poverty, low education, lack of employment opportunities, gender discrimination and conflict, amongst other reasons, for wanting to migrate abroad. Usually, trafficking victims and smuggled persons make the choice to leave their homes, whether as economic migrants, asylum seekers or to be reunited with their families, among many other reasons (Buckland 2009). Indeed, as Gregoriou and Ras emphasise,

this distinction also distracts from the fact that both smuggled and trafficked people are often vulnerable, escaping a local environment plagued by poverty, conflict, disaster, or all of the above, searching, despite the many risks involved, for a better place in which to live and work. (2018: 5)

Whilst the motivation to migrate is often the same, the ultimate determination of the migrant's 'smuggled' or 'trafficked' status often results from being able to afford less risky means of travelling or can result from responses to the sort of unplanned coincidences that occur on complex migrant journeys.

The key distinguishing characteristics in international law are the transnational component, the financial considerations, the methods of transport and the relationship between the victim and the trafficker/smuggler. Key to effectively distinguishing between smuggling and trafficking is establishing what knowledge, if any, the potential victims possessed at the beginning the process. In conventional cases that do not divert from the Protocol definitions, a smuggled person knows they are being smuggled at the point of departure, whilst a trafficked victim does not know that they are to be exploited.

However, this distinction can be readily blurred. There are some clear examples of trafficking such as a child kidnapped without parental consent or of SOM where migrant workers 'hire' a smuggler to cross a state border. Yet, often the distinction is less perceptible and, at multiple junctures along the journey, it might be unclear whether there is consent or not, whether the migrant is being smuggled or trafficked. Some undocumented migrants might consent in some way to the initial proposition to travel; however, during the journey or on arrival in the destination state, circumstances may change markedly.

The lack of consent to a situation of exploitation is integral to the crime of trafficking and, through the operation of the means element, has been accepted as a distinct and important part of the definition of human trafficking (UNODC 2014). The definition in Article 3(b) of the Trafficking Protocol makes clear that consent of the victim to the intended exploitation is irrelevant when any of these means have been used. Victims may initially give consent to be trafficked, but this will be negated if the trafficker used any of the means to obtain it. A trafficked person cannot consent to being trafficked, and any consent given is not applicable if the victim was not able to give it freely. Children under 18 cannot consent to exploitation, and any child recruited, transported or transferred for the purposes of exploitation is considered a potential victim of trafficking, whether or not they are forced or deceived. Children are not deemed capable in international law of giving informed consent, and therefore consent is not relevant.

Human trafficking is a crime against the person because it is a violation of the victim's human rights, and a criminal offence is being perpetrated against the victim. Human trafficking is both transnational and national. Victims can be moved across borders either legally or illegally using the victim's documents or false documents, or they can be trafficked within the borders of their own or another state. People who are smuggled, however, enter into a commercial agreement with the smuggler voluntarily and consent to the undertaking even if they are placed in danger or suffer degrading conditions. This agreement is a contractual arrangement whereby the smuggled person agrees to pay the smuggler for the services provided. SOM is a crime against the State, there is no victim and it is a breach of immigration laws. It can only be transnational as the objective is to facilitate an illegal border crossing to gain entry to another state. If the migrant's own documentation prevents the legal crossing of borders, smugglers will provide false or stolen documents for a fee. They will have freedom of movement and are able to leave the smuggling situation if they choose to do so. Victims of human trafficking, conversely, do not consent to being trafficked and cannot agree to be exploited. They are commodities obtained by trafficking that can be bought and sold without their agreement and who have no genuine freedom of movement. Moreover, ultimately, the profits in SOM are made from the fees received for transporting people illegally across borders to their ultimate destination, whereas profits in human trafficking are made when the victim is exploited.

States need to ensure that there are proper identification procedures to be able to differentiate between trafficked victims and smuggled migrants. Sufficient time should be permitted to make a safe identification to avoid potential trafficked victims being deported before any identification can take place. The complexities involved in distinguishing between human trafficking and SOM means victims of trafficking may be mistaken for illegal migrants, miscategorised by authorities and potentially deported without proper assistance. This often leads to further victimisation and allows the traffickers to remain unpunished (Batsyukova 2012).

Article 16 of the SOM Protocol sets out protection and assistance measures that each State Party should undertake to be consistent with international law. This includes taking all appropriate measures to preserve the 'the right to life and the right not to be subjected to torture or other cruel, inhuman or degrading treatment or punishment'. However, protection under the SOM Protocol falls well short of the protection afforded to trafficking victims by the Trafficking Protocol. Consequently, it is with justification that Jacqueline Bhabha and Monette Zard conclude that 'there is much to be gained from being classified as trafficked, and much to lose from being considered smuggled' (2006: 7). As Svitlana Batsyukova cautions, 'the two phenomena are inter-related, and proper identification may take time…the use of a sensitive, humane and informed approach at the point of identification of irregular migrants is of upmost importance' (2012: 47).

Triage: Trafficked Victims or Illegal Migrants

As discussed above, the effectiveness of criminal justice responses, whether targeting the criminal enterprises involved in trafficking or seeking to mitigate the demand for products of exploitation, can have an effect on the human trafficking business model which currently thrives because perceived rewards significantly outweigh perceived risks. There are a number of challenges to an effective criminal justice response. However, a fundamental problem is that many cases are simply not identified. A lack of clear identification mechanisms and guidelines is often compounded by limited incentives for victims to come forward in terms of both the access to the criminal justice system and the limited protection and welfare assistance available to victims.

There is no victim stereotype and victims have no common characteristics. The profile of a victim can be influenced by the form of exploitation involved and vulnerabilities inextricably linked to, and shaped by, the dynamics of contemporary global migration. Thus, efforts by law enforcement and border agencies to profile victims have had mixed results. An Australian study found that profiling by border agencies is being used to deport sex workers trying to enter the country even if they are being trafficked, commenting that 'while the border is a poor site for identifying cases of trafficking into the sex industry, it is a site of significant social sorting, where various intersections of intelligence-led profiling and everyday stereotyping of women, sex work and vulnerability play out' (Pickering and Ham 2013: 17). Since the offence of human trafficking is completed once a trafficker recruits a potential victim with the *intention* to exploit, the crime may have already been committed when individuals, not yet exploited but whose exploitation is planned, present at the border.

A key juncture for trafficked persons is when they first come into direct contact with the authorities of the state into which, or in which, they are being trafficked that might include border agencies, law enforcement or health and welfare institutions. At other stages of the trafficking process, victims might be identified by representatives of NGOs or international organisations, concerned citizens or other victims. These junctures represent critical points in the trafficking process where accurate identification can lead to a positive or negative outcome for the victim. The nature of the assistance and protection needed by trafficked victims often differs from that required by other migrants. Trafficked victims are liable to have immediate and acute physical, sexual and psychological health needs. As victims of serious crimes, specific security arrangements and procedures are necessary, not least because agency personnel assisting victims can themselves be exposed to risk.

The prompt identification of potential victims of human trafficking is important to ensure that victims receive the protection to which they are entitled to and that investigations and prosecutions can be undertaken. Indicators can be objective and subjective, primary and secondary. However, all indicators being used for identification need to be understood by those making identification decisions. There are numerous forms of human trafficking, as well as new and emerging forms of exploitation. The identification of victims requires knowledge not only of the trafficking process but also of the distinction between human trafficking and SOM. As noted above, this distinction is itself problematic, not so much at the level of the Protocols, but at the level of domestic legislation and, in particular, in the specific cultural and social context of implementation. As Julietta Hua and Holly Nigorizawa explain, 'only those who are able to prove their authenticity by fitting into pre-existing assumptions tied to the category "trafficked victim" are officially granted victim status' (2010: 402). The identification process can be time-consuming because of the complexity of the crime and the criminal networks involved. Human trafficking is a hidden crime, and victims are often unaware of their rights or do not understand the laws of the state into which, or in which, they are being trafficked (OSCE 2014: 48–50). More fundamentally, trafficked victims are often unaware they are being trafficked and are mistrustful of the authorities, and hence do not seek assistance.

Ineffective identification methodologies, together with emerging, and as yet unrecognised, forms of trafficking mean that many victims are not categorised as such. In some states, trafficking for sexual exploitation is seen as the principal, or only, type of human trafficking, and forced labour is not adequately understood, recognised or identified. Likewise, where facilities exist to protect and support victims, these are aimed at victims of sex trafficking, often women rather than men, rather than victims of labour trafficking. Even where some support exists, this often does not continue after the period of reflection required by a referral mechanism is complete, leading to the potential for re-trafficking.

The process of identification aims to determine whether an individual is potentially a trafficked person according to the definitions of human trafficking established in international and/or domestic legal instruments. Victims should be identified as quickly as possible to remove them from the position of exploitation, to assist with their immediate physical and psychological needs, and to provide appropriate protection measures. Clause 16 of the United Nations Declaration of Basic Principles of Justice for Victims of Crime and Abuse of Power (1985) states that those people who are likely to be in contact with victims of trafficking should receive adequate training to assist them in identifying and responding sensitively to their needs. Further, Article 10 of the CoE Convention requires that

> each Party shall provide its competent authorities with persons who are trained and qualified in preventing and combating trafficking in human beings, in identifying and helping victims, including children, and shall ensure that the different authorities collaborate with each other as well as with relevant support organisations.

Whilst states' responses to human trafficking are far from universal, the OSCE has produced a set of guidelines for interviewing potential victims, intended to steer practice amongst the 57 mainly developed world states that make up its membership (see Box 2.1).

Indicators for the identification of victims of human trafficking can be behavioural, physical or circumstantial. These may be general or specific to a discrete form of human trafficking. Indicators are further divided into objective indicators based on observation and subjective indicators determined through interviews and investigation. Indicators remain, however, merely indicative rather than conclusive evidence that an individual has been trafficked. Nonetheless, the presence of indicators should require the relevant agencies to initiate further investigation.

Box 2.1   Standard operating procedure for the formal identification of trafficked victims

The suggested procedure for the formal identification of victims of trafficking in human beings in the current framework of first reception and identification centres for refugees and migrants in the OSCE region constitutes the following steps:

1. As soon as a field professional identifies a presumed victim of trafficking in human beings, the respective Agency 'Combatting Trafficking in Human Beings (CTHB) Focal Point' should be notified and informed of the profile of the presumed victim (e.g., gender, age, spoken language). The Agency CTHB Focal Point then should notify the local CTHB Co-ordinator and pass on the available information about the presumed victim's profile.

2. The local CTHB Co-ordinator, based on the presumed victim's initial profile, should communicate with the relevant services, including transportation, interpretation/cultural mediation, and accommodation, to make all of the necessary arrangements. While these arrangements are being made, the presumed victim should be offered a safe, quiet, and private space provided by the respective referral agency.

3. The referral agency CTHB Focal Point should accompany the presumed victim to her/his safe accommodation and address the presumed victim's immediate basic needs, including providing the presumed victim with information about identification procedures and the rights of victims of trafficking in human beings. Provisions should be made to ensure the presumed victim's access to all necessary medical and psychological support.

4. As soon as the presumed victim is settled and her/his basic needs have been addressed, a second-line interview should be carried out by a trained second-line interviewer(s) in a safe space that ensures privacy. If the presumed victim does not wish to be interviewed by a law enforcement representative, the second-line interview should be conducted by a trained welfare professional only.

5. It is suggested that the second-line interview be carried out by two professionals (either one law enforcement officer and one welfare professional, or two welfare professionals). If necessary, an interpreter and a cultural mediator should also be present. Interviews with presumed child victims of human trafficking should be conducted in the presence of the legal guardian they have been assigned. If needed, the interview may be stopped and resumed later due to the mental or physical state of the presumed victim.

6. If it is planned to audio-record the interview, the presumed victim should be asked for her/his consent to this.

(continued)

Box 2.1 (continued)

7. After the second-line interview is completed, the presumed victim should be accompanied back to her/his safe accommodation and continue to receive all necessary medical and psychological support.
8. The data collected during the second-line interview should be communicated to the local CTHB Co-ordinator in the form of a report compiled by the second-line interviewer(s).
9. If the presumed victim wishes to acquire the status of victim of trafficking in human beings and has given her/his consent to collaborate with law enforcement authorities, the local CTHB Co-ordinator should take the case to the local Multi-Agency Committee, which should then take a decision on the attribution of status.
10. If the presumed victim wishes to acquire the status of victim of trafficking in human beings, but has not given her/his consent to collaborate with law enforcement authorities, the local CTHB Co-ordinator should still communicate the case to the local Multi-Agency Committee. In such cases, law enforcement authorities should also be informed of the circumstances of the case, but without being given access to the presumed victim's personal data. They should consider investigating the case without involving the presumed victim.
11. The attribution of the status of victim of trafficking in human beings should activate an in-depth needs assessment procedure that aims at establishing the victim's immediate and long-term needs. The results of this needs assessment should serve as a basis for a case-specific protection and assistance plan developed by welfare professionals. Unified needs assessment tools should be developed to support this procedure. If the plan requires special protection measures, such measures should be developed and implemented by law enforcement authorities.
12. If the presumed victim does not wish to acquire the status of victim of trafficking in human beings, the local CTHB Co-ordinator should file the case and liaise with the RIC CTHB Focal Point. The presumed victim should be transported to and accommodated at the RIC, where she/he should continue to receive assistance as a vulnerable individual.

Source: OSCE (2019)

Indicators are used in multisectoral circumstances to determine 'what is potentially happening'. It is not necessary that all indicators are satisfied. They open the door for secondary, more specific, investigation to take place. As law enforcement strategies have developed, the use of indicators has increased, and international organisations and individual states have published guidelines listing both general and specific indicators. In 2009, the UNODC produced a manual for criminal justice practitioners listing general indicators for human trafficking, as well as lists of indicators for specific forms of human trafficking including child trafficking, sex trafficking, trafficking for domestic servitude, labour trafficking and trafficking for the purpose of begging or committing petty crimes (UNODC 2009).

Exploitation

The purpose of human trafficking is the exploitation of the victim. However, whilst exploitation as an element of the crime is important, it is also problematic. Exploitation is not defined in the Trafficking Protocol and the onus is on states to provide a definition. Article 3 (a) of the Trafficking Protocol states that 'exploitation shall include, at a minimum, the exploitation or the prostitution of others or other forms of sexual exploitation, forced labour or services, slavery practices similar to slavery, servitude or the removal of organs'. Article 2 of the Trafficking Directive adopts a broader notion of what should be considered human trafficking and includes additional forms of exploitation. These are 'forced begging' which should be understood as a form of forced labour and the 'exploitation of criminal activities' which should be understood as the exploitation of a person to commit, *inter alia,* pick-pocketing, shop-lifting, drug trafficking and other criminal activities which are subject to penalties and imply financial gain. However, it should be stressed that the act of human trafficking is complete before any exploitation occurs. It is the trafficker's purpose to exploit, not the actual exploitation that completes the third element of the crime of human trafficking.

The UNODC (2015) acknowledge that exploitation is not well, or uniformly, understood, and the absence of clear definitions in the law—both of exploitation and of stipulated forms of exploitation—raises practical and evidentiary challenges to investigations and prosecutions. Such considerations are especially relevant in relation to forms of exploitation that particularly affect women and girls such as domestic servitude and forced or servile marriage. Indeed, in many cultures, the exploitation of women migrant workers has been 'normalised' to the point that it is not generally recognised as trafficking.

Exploitation is not a *function* of human trafficking, but the ultimate goal of the trafficker that provides the incentive for each step of the trafficking process. As Conny Rijken points out,

> exploitation can, for instance, also exist in bad living conditions, bad working conditions, long working hours, or another violation of labour laws. In some countries any violation of labour law is sufficient to qualify as exploitation, thus not requiring a means or involuntariness. However, one has to keep in mind that the existence of exploitation does not necessarily mean that [human trafficking] for labour exploitation exists, as for the existence of [human trafficking] the other two elements, namely, an act and means are also required. (Rijken 2013: 18)

Hence, whilst exploitation is an essential element of human trafficking, understanding the meaning of exploitation has been problematic because the onus is on each state to provide a definition.

For example, in the context of the UK and/or England and Wales, successive statutes avoid directly defining exploitation. Section 145 of the Nationality, Immigration and Asylum Act (2002) does not define exploitation but refers to the offence of prostitution only. This statute was replaced by sections 57–60 of the Sexual Offences Act 2003 which again provide no definition of exploitation, but rather refers to the 'commission of the relevant offence' and provides a wider definition of the offences that could be committed under the legislation. Section 4 of the Asylum and Immigration (Treatment of Claimants etc.) Act (2004) was the first legislation to refer to exploitation and states the circumstances under which a person can be exploited for the purpose of the offence. The Modern Slavery Act (2015) claims to give a meaning of exploitation stating that 'for the purposes of section 2 a person is exploited only if one or more of the following subsections apply in relation to the person'. These subsections, however, fall short of defining exploitation, but rather set out the circumstances in which a person is exploited for the purposes of the offence.

Forms of exploitation are proliferating (see Box 2.2) and victims can be exploited in more than one way. Chuang refers to the shift within international law from 'forced labour' to 'human trafficking', and more recently from 'human trafficking' to 'modern slavery' as 'exploitation creep' (2014).

Box 2.2   Typology of modern slavery offences in the UK

Labour exploitation
- Victims exploited for multiple purposes in isolated environments
- Victims work for offenders
- Victims work for someone other than offenders

Domestic servitude
- Exploited by partner
- Exploited by relatives
- Exploiters not related to victims

Sexual exploitation
- Child Sexual Exploitation – group exploitation
- Child Sexual Exploitation – single exploiter
- Forced sex work in fixed location
- Forced sex work in changing location
- Trafficking for personal gratification

Criminal exploitation
- Forced gang-related criminality
- Forced labour in illegal activities
- Forced acquisitive crime
- Forced begging
- Trafficking for forced sham marriage
- Financial fraud (including benefit fraud)

Source: Home Office (2017), 'A typology of modern slavery offences in the UK'. London: Home Office

Notwithstanding, it is realistic to expect that different forms of exploitation will continue to be identified and designated as trafficking offences and that individuals will be trafficked into these exploitative situations by traffickers for profit. Exploitation is the source of profit in human trafficking cases and the motivation for traffickers to carry out their crime. Exploitation may take a range of forms, but there remains the assumption that the more the productive labour traffickers can extract from victims, the larger the financial incentive to carry out the crime.

The absence of a definition of exploitation in the Trafficking Protocol and other international legal instruments means that individual states have the capacity to stipulate forms of exploitation. States can add new forms of human trafficking or interpret undefined forms in a way that captures conduct relevant in a given country or cultural context (UNODC 2015). In particular, the forms of exploitation involved in labour exploitation are becoming increasingly complex and often ambiguous. The OSCE emphasises that this can lead to intrinsic problems for the investigation of human trafficking for labour exploitation.

> Cases of trafficking for forced labour are difficult to identify, in part because exploited workers are often reluctant to identify themselves as victims, preferring to work in poor conditions rather than return to their home countries, and because there is a lack of definition [at EU level] of the degree of exploitation serious enough to constitute a crime. A lack of awareness and capability of making the distinction between an employment dispute and a case of trafficking can result in a form of serious crime being dealt with as a local labour issue with possible negative consequences for the migrant/ illegal worker. (OSCE 2013b: 62)

As well as emerging forms of exploitation, traffickers also evolve their *modus operandi*. Those tasked with investigating human trafficking often experience difficulty in separating bad working conditions from situations that should be pursued as trafficking offences. In practice, whilst often not a relevant consideration under the law, severity in the amount of force used or the nature of the deception can be relevant to establishing exploitation at both the investigative and prosecutorial stages. Likewise, cultural and national contexts and indigenous perceptions often ultimately determine what local law enforcement and criminal justice agencies pursue, or do not pursue, as exploitation in any particular instance. Understanding these cultural determinants can be as important as understanding the different forms of exploitation.

A study by Ella Cockbain and Kate Bowers based on data from the UK's central system for identifying trafficking victims confirms that there exist 'important and often nuanced distinctions between those trafficked for sex, labour and domestic servitude' (2019: 27). That different forms of exploitation are recognised within different states can obstruct the prosecution of cases and the protection of victims. The divergence in states' definitions can have a chilling effect on prosecutions relying on interstate collaboration through the type of MLA envisaged by the UNTOC (UNODC 2004b). Likewise, whether a particular form of exploitation constitutes the criminal offence of human trafficking in a given state has an impact on whether or not protection is offered to the exploited person since mandatory protection is only available to those designated victims of human trafficking.

Conclusion

Whilst the distinction between human trafficking and SOM is explicit in the Protocols, in practice, distinguishing between the crimes is far from straightforward. Yet, whether an individual is identified as a trafficked victim or a smuggled migrant fundamentally determines her/his future treatment. The morality, and practicality, of the distinction between smuggling and trafficking, especially how this is understood at the level of implementation, needs more attention at scholarly, practitioner and policy levels. There is evidence that determining status at key junctures, for example at borders, fails to accurately establish the exploitative trajectory of the individual migrant journey.

The current distinction in international law, and the interpretation of this distinction at national level, inevitably leads to the victim/criminal dichotomy between trafficked/smuggled migrants. However, this more fundamental question does not diminish the reality that individuals who are being trafficked are victims of a serious crime, and aside from help and support, need to be removed from criminal harm without delay. States are under a duty to put in place human resources tasked with making a prompt and accurate identification of trafficked victims. Identification can, however, be hindered by the complexity of human trafficking as a crime, the psychological and physical constraints placed on victims by traffickers, reticence on the part of victims to cooperate with the authorities and constantly evolving methods and forms of trafficking.

Consent and agency lie at the heart of distinguishing between trafficking and SOM. To determine whether trafficking has taken place, those making the identification should have specialist training in order to distinguish indicators specific to increasingly distinct forms of trafficking and be able to make subjective judgments based on detailed interviews. A further impediment to identifying trafficked victims is the imprecision of the concept of 'exploitation' in the Trafficking Protocol. What constitutes a type, or degree, of exploitation that reaches the threshold of criminal trafficking is determined by domestic law and/or interpreted by law enforcement agencies working within divergent and particular cultural circumstances. This divergence in defining exploitation can be manipulated by traffickers to their advantage, but can also hinder transnational investigations and prosecutions.

References

Batsyukova, S. (2012), 'Human trafficking and human smuggling: similar nature, different concepts', *Studies of Changing Societies: Comparative and Interdisciplinary Focus* Vol. 1 No. 1.

Bhabha, J. and Zard, M. (2006), 'Human Smuggling and Trafficking: the good, the bad and the ugly', *Forced Migration Review* no. 25, May.

Brian, T., and Laczko, F. (2014), Fatal Journeys: Tracking Lives Lost during Migration, Geneva: IOM.

Buckland, B. (2009). 'Human Trafficking and Smuggling: Crossover and Overlap', in Friesendorf, C. (ed.), *Strategies Against Human Trafficking: The Role of the Security Sector*, Vienna and Geneva: National Defence Academy and Austrian Ministry of Defence and Sports.

Chuang, J. (2014), 'Exploitation Creep and the Unmaking of Human Trafficking Law, *American Journal of International Law,* Vol. 108, No. 4.

Cockbain, E., and Bowers, K. (2019), 'Human trafficking for sex, labour and domestic servitude: how do key trafficking types compare and what are their predictors?', Crime, Law and Social Change, Vol. 72, No. 1.

Ferrier, T., and Kaminsky, P. (2017), 'An industry built on human misery', June. Available at https://www.mindsglobalspotlight.com/2017/06/01/32072/global-spotlight-the-overview.

Gregoriou, C., and Ras, I. (2018), 'Representations of Transnational Human Trafficking: A Critical Review', in Gregoriou, C. (ed.), *Representations of Transnational Human Trafficking: Present-day News Media, True Crime and Fiction*. Basingstoke: Palgrave Pivot.

Home Office (2017), 'A typology of modern slavery offences in the UK'. London: Home Office. Available at https://www.gov.uk/government/uploads/system/uploads/attachment_data/file/652652/typology-modern-slavery-offences-horr93.pdf.

Hua, J., and Nigorizawa, H. (2010), 'US sex trafficking, women's human rights and the politics of representation', *International Feminist Journal of Politics*, Vol. 12, Nos. 3–4.

International Labour Organisation (2014), *Profits and Poverty: The Economics of Forced Labour*. Geneva: ILO.

Organization for Security and Cooperation in Europe (2013b), 'OSCE Resource Police Training Guide: Trafficking in Human Beings', SPMU Publication Series, Vol. 10.

Organization for Security and Cooperation in Europe (2014), *National Referral Mechanisms: Joining Efforts to Protect the Rights of Trafficked Persons A Practical Handbook*. Warsaw: OSCE Office for Democratic Institutions and Human Rights.

Organization for Security and Cooperation in Europe (2019), *Uniform Guidelines for the Identification and Referral of Victims of Human Trafficking within the Migrant and Refugee Reception Framework in the OSCE Region*, Vienna: OSCE/Office of the Special Representative and Co-ordinator for Combating Trafficking in Human Beings. Available at https://www.osce.org/files/f/documents/2/4/413123_0.pdf.

Pickering, S., and Ham, J. (2013), 'Hot Pants at the Border: Sorting Sex Work from Trafficking', *British Journal of Criminology*, Vol. 54, No. 1.

Rijken, C. (2013), 'Trafficking in Human Beings for Labour Exploitation: Cooperation in an Integrated Approach', *European Journal of Crime, Criminal Law and Criminal Justice*, Vol. 21, No. 1.

United Nations Office on Drugs and Crime (2009), *Anti-human trafficking manual for criminal justice practitioners*. Vienna: UNODC.

United Nations Office on Drugs and Crime (2018), Global Study on Smuggling of Migrants. Vienna: UNODC.

United Nations Office on Drugs and Crime (2012) *International Framework for Action to Implement the Smuggling of Migrants Trafficking Protocol*. Vienna: UNODC.

United Nations Office on Drugs and Crime (2004b), *UN Convention Against Transnational Crime and the Trafficking Protocols Thereto*. Vienna: UNODC.

United Nations Office on Drugs and Crime (2015), 'The Concept of 'Exploitation' in the Trafficking in Persons Trafficking Protocol', *UNODC Issue Paper*. Available at https://www.unodc.org/documents/congress/background-information/Human_Trafficking/UNODC_2015_Issue_Paper_Exploitation.pdf.

United Nations Office on Drugs and Crime (2014), 'The Role of 'Consent' in the Trafficking in Persons Trafficking Protocol', *UNODC Issue Paper*. Available at https://www.unodc.org/documents/human-trafficking/2014/UNODC_2014_Issue_Paper_Consent.pdf.

3

Pursuing Human Traffickers

Abstract The investigation and prosecution of traffickers is an obligation both as a moral imperative and to deter future offending. Investigation is costly in terms of physical and human resources, requiring law enforcement agents trained in, often invasive, specialist investigative techniques and working closely with criminal justice practitioners. A further layer of complexity is provided by financial investigation including forensic accountancy to enable potential asset seizing. International law places the victim at the heart of investigation and prosecution. However, victim protection, requiring sensitive case management, brings practical challenges that can limit the number and success of prosecutions. The UK has been pivotal to the EU's counter-trafficking strategy, and Brexit is likely to damage the capacity of British and, to a lesser extent, European agencies to investigate and prosecute trafficking cases.

Keywords: Investigation • Prosecution • Victim-centred • Protection • Brexit

© The Author(s) 2020
S. Massey, G. Rankin, *Exploiting People for Profit*,
https://doi.org/10.1057/978-1-137-43413-5_3

Countering human trafficking depends on international cooperation between law enforcement and criminal justice agencies. The definition of human trafficking in the Trafficking Protocol recognises that the crime, and the associated transportation of victims, might take place entirely within the territory of a single sovereign state. However, many instances of human trafficking have a transnational dimension, and victims, witnesses and defendants can all, potentially, be from different states and located in different states. Moreover, the offence itself might have taken place in another state. Whilst international cooperation can be challenging due to legal, cultural, political and language differences, there are legal rules and procedures to facilitate cooperation and the tools required to prosecute traffickers. The UNTOC contains detailed provisions on both formal and informal cooperation in criminal matters, which are also applicable, *mutatis mutandis*, to the Trafficking Protocol.

The chapter is divided into three sections. The first section considers the potential strategic approaches to investigating human trafficking crimes available to law enforcement investigators. The chapter then moves on to explore the complexities of prosecution concentrating on the responsibility to keep the victim at the centre of the trial process, even when, for legitimate reasons, the victim might be unwilling to cooperate with the prosecution. Finally, whilst surveying the strategies and tools available to EU member states to cooperate in investigating and prosecuting serious crime, the final section will assess the impact of the withdrawal of the UK from the EU on Britain's capacity to effectively counter human trafficking.

Investigating Human Trafficking

Investigating human trafficking cases is a complex process involving victims and witnesses frequently reluctant to report potential cases and often unable or unwilling to cooperate with law enforcement and criminal justice agencies. A high proportion of investigations involve transnational crimes that require evidence to be gathered from different states necessitating international cooperation and MLA. Trafficking within a state can also be problematic requiring information sharing between regional policing and prosecution agencies.

All investigations should be victim-centred, respecting the human rights of the victim. No action should be taken that could put a victim at risk and it is for this reason that the development of specialist investigative techniques is required. Investigators need to consider the possibility of victimless prosecutions and the validity of disruption as an investigative strategy if it is in the best interests of the victim. They need to know how to identify, interview and protect victims. They also need to discover the specific issues that confront victims including the nature of the trauma involved and why victims might be unable or unwilling to give evidence. In practice, all victims of human trafficking are entitled to the following standards: a respect for their human rights, protection and safety, individualised care, the right to self-determination, full Information and consent, the right to non-discrimination, and confidentiality.

There are numerous significant challenges to investigating human trafficking cases and a number of potential barriers. Victims may be traumatised, in fear, or just want the money they are owed. Human trafficking is a clandestine crime and victims are often unwilling or unable to cooperate and reluctant to report the crime. Transnational cases require evidence to be obtained from different states, often involving the use of MLA. Investigators need to know the options available to them, understand why victims and witnesses do not wish to cooperate, how to prosecute successfully and why financial investigations are important.

There are three main approaches to investigating cases of human trafficking. When specific information has been received that either an offence has been committed or there is a potential victim in in need of rescue, and following due diligence and risk assessment, a *reactive* investigation is instigated. These investigations are immediate and can be initiated by a complaint from a victim or information from a member of the public. Reactive investigations result from a clear duty for states to respond to known instances of trafficking, especially if the potential victim is a child. These investigations include the gathering of corroborative evidence, interviewing victims and suspects, obtaining statements, analysing materials recovered, and preparing a case for trial. Reactive investigations might be unavoidable if victims are in immediate physical danger.

However, 'such tactics make it difficult to set up longer-term undercover operations, conduct surveillance, or develop the type of intelligence needed to understand trafficking networks and operations' (Farrell and Pfeffer 2014: 55).

Pro-active investigations based on intelligence are better planned and structured. The objective of the investigation is to rescue victims and/or to obtain evidence that will enable the arrest and prosecution of those responsible for the trafficking. Traditionally, these are the most successful and effective operations, notably in the case of sexual exploitation. Being intelligence-led, pro-active investigations enable law enforcement agencies to surveil the location of the criminal activity identifying both criminals and victims. Without the time constraints of a reactive investigation, pro-active investigations aim to construct a cohesive relationship between law enforcement and criminal justice agencies to ensure a successful prosecution and conviction based on admissible evidence. However, in the context of human trafficking investigations across 12 US counties, Amy Farrell and Rebecca Pfeffer report that 'detectives we interviewed believed there was little they could do to pro-actively find human trafficking cases; instead, they waited for victims to come forward to police or to other service providers who could make referrals to the police' (2014: 54). The effectiveness of the law enforcement response to human trafficking links with the policy priorities of individual state jurisdictions. Farrell, Vanessa Bouché and Dana Wolfe find that there is a correlation between '[states] funding victim services, training law enforcement, and supporting multidisciplinary task forces activated to respond to human trafficking cases' and the proportion of successful prosecutions (2019: 190). Moreover,

> states that passed legal provisions to enhance investigative and prosecutorial tools also saw higher numbers of state arrests and prosecutions of human trafficking suspects, likely because they promote pro-active investigations and support victims through long prosecution processes. (Farrell et al. 2019: 190)

Disruptive investigations aim to interrupt criminal activities and may be used when reactive and pro-active investigations are not either possible or appropriate. This tactic is valuable when there is insufficient evidence for a reactive or pro-active investigation, but a clear need to address a pressing case of human trafficking, possibly in circumstances where surveillance and/or undercover investigation are not practicable; where there is no legal basis for a reactive or pro-active investigation and/or where resources are not available for a wider investigation. The disruptive response is faster than a pro-active investigation, yet has the potential to generate intelligence which may lead to a pro-active investigation.

Intelligence, defined as information that has been collected, collated, analysed and evaluated, is used to collect information and knowledge on the perpetrators of trafficking and how they operate. It provides the knowledge and understanding to identify and inform operational decisions and to select the best subjects for a pro-active investigation. Intelligence-led policing (ILP) has been likened to 'a business model and managerial philosophy where data analysis and crime intelligence are pivotal to an objective decision-making framework that facilitates crime and problem reduction, disruption and prevention through both the strategic management and effective enforcement strategies that target serious and prolific offenders' (Ratcliffe 2008: 6). Intelligence gathering may be divided into two types. The objective of strategic intelligence is to conduct an overall intelligence assessment of the various strategic factors that underpin the phenomenon of human trafficking. Tactical intelligence affords immediate and timely support to ongoing investigations by identifying offenders and by providing advance information on their movements. It leads to specific action, including arrests, further investigations and prosecution (UNODC 2014a).

In order to effectively manage the complexity of most human trafficking crimes, law enforcement agencies need to employ specialist investigative techniques (SITs). Article 20 of UNTOC which deals with SIT provides for 'the appropriate use of controlled delivery' and 'the use of other special investigative techniques, such as electronic or other forms of surveillance and undercover operations'. These techniques should be employed only by the competent authorities and should be legal under the domestic law of the relevant State Party. Further, States Parties are 'encouraged to conclude, when necessary, appropriate bilateral or multilateral agreements or arrangements for using such special investigative techniques in the context of cooperation at the international level'. In the absence of such an agreement, the use of SIT should be made on a case-by-case basis.

SITs are often held by investigators and prosecutors to be crucial components of pro-active investigations and are used to obtain high-quality evidence that can be used to identify victims, traffickers and their *modus operandi*, as well as the location of the exploitation. Intrinsically intrusive, these techniques should only be undertaken by trained law enforcement officers when necessary and proportionate. SIT can be used individually or in a combination depending on the requirements of the investigation. The difficulties attached to mounting a prosecution for human trafficking have led to calls from some international organisations, such as Interpol and the UNODC, for wider use of SIT. However, this trend is contested by Gallagher and Paul Holmes who argue that, 'even in countries where resources and skills permit an adequate pro-active response, such techniques generally do not supply the evidence necessary to secure convictions of traffickers' (2008: 332).

Article 27.1 of the CoE Convention states that investigations should not be dependent upon a report or accusation by the victim and that criminal proceedings should continue even if the victim has withdrawn her/his statement. This would seem to necessitate the use and development of investigative techniques that do not rely on victim evidence and can provide compelling evidence, when corroborated, even if a victim is unwilling or unable to give evidence enabling a case to continue. However, SIT is expensive, requiring human and technical resources usually only available in developed world states. Gallagher and Holmes reiterate their position that the victim, and appropriate victim support, should sit at the heart of the investigation of human trafficking cases (2008).

> National criminal justice agencies should be working toward a situation whereby victims of trafficking are recognised as an essential resource and are provided with the protections and incentives they require to participate in the prosecution of their exploiters. (2008: 332)

The most widely cited figures for the profitability of human trafficking remain the ILO's 2012 estimates published in 2014. The estimated profits of human trafficking amount to $150 billion each year, of which $99 billion comes from commercial sexual exploitation and a further $51 billion from forced economic exploitation (ILO 2014: 13–15). Since the main motivation of all traffickers is to make money from their criminal enterprises, countering human trafficking requires effective financial investigation (FI) to seize the illegally obtained assets of the traffickers. Article 6 of the UNTOC provides for the 'criminalisation of the laundering of proceeds of crime' and Article 8 of the UNTOC provides for 'measures to combat money-laundering'. An FI can corroborate the evidence collected in the main criminal investigation, and the FI in human trafficking cases should, legislation permitting, commence at the same time as that of the criminal investigation.

An FI traces the profits derived from human trafficking, profits that also allow exploitation to continue. An FI also enables funds to be seized, confiscated, forfeited, restrained or frozen as proceeds of crime. It can target the financial gains acquired by the traffickers and provide effective remedies to sequestrating these gains through a number of divergent solutions. These investigations use the same methods and specialist techniques as criminal investigations to prove that money was obtained illegally through the exploitation of victims. Once it can be established that the traffickers' assets are a result of criminal activity, then application can be made for the appropriate financial remedies. To date, however, asset seizures from human traffickers have been limited. Based on data from ten states in Europe, Asia and the Pacific, and Central and South America, the UNODC reports that 'the yearly amounts [of confiscated assets] vary greatly from a few thousands to $6m' (UNODC 2014b: 53). Moreover, 'when the confiscated funds are compared to the number of detected victims the funds remain below $9,000 per victim; in most cases below $2,000 per victim' (UNODC 2014b: 53). The UNODC and the Financial Action Task Force (FATF), an intergovernmental body comprised of states that host major financial centres, have proposed that 'law enforcement should concentrate on the financial aspect of the crime, focusing more on financial investigations than on the predicate offence of human trafficking' (Messer 2019: 1).

The FI has the advantage of providing restitution to victims and potentially uncovering the wider networks involved in instance of human trafficking. However, fundamentally, 'it is the seizure of assets that many believe will help turn human trafficking from a low-risk, high-reward crime to one that offenders do not see the benefit of participating in due to increased incarceration and the loss of assets' (Messer 2019: 2). Given the specific circumstances of human trafficking crimes, the advantages of FI in the majority of human trafficking cases may be conjectural, 'in reality…these theoretical advantages are diluted by practical considerations as the outlook of human trafficking does not lend itself well to financial investigation' (Middleton et al. 2019: 293). Arguably, at least in the UK context, human trafficking is fragmented, often small scale, embedded in legal businesses, and 'sophisticated laundering schemes are the exception rather than the rule'; therefore, most cases are better addressed by law enforcement 'using older, more established and better known methods' (Middleton et al. 2019: 293).

In the context of investigations within the European Union, a joint investigation team (JIT) can be set up consisting of judges, prosecutors and law enforcement officers established for a fixed period and a specific purpose by way of a written agreement between states to carry out criminal investigations in one or more states. Emphasising the importance of JITs in investigating and prosecuting serious crimes, Keir Starmer, then Director of Public Prosecutions, stated to the UK Parliament's EU Committee that JITs allow for speedier cross-border coordination, the deployment of UK law enforcement authorities to other member states, the provision of direct access to the same evidence for all member states and the increased admissibility of evidence, previously often challenged before the courts (ATMG 2017: 9). The possibility of setting up JITs between member states is provided for in Article 13 of the Mutual Legal Assistance Convention (2000) and the EU Framework Decision on JITs. These teams allow information to be shared without the need for a formal request. Requests for investigative and coercive measures can be made directly between team members, dispensing with the need for 'letters rogatory' or formal requests for assistance from foreign courts. Advantages of JITs are the sharing of evidence through the presence of team members at house searches and interviews, the coordination of investigative efforts *in situ,* the informal exchange of specialised knowledge, the building of mutual trust between practitioners from different jurisdictions, and the development of optimal investigation and prosecution strategies. Finally, JITs allow for Europol and Eurojust to be involved in an investigation, providing the direct support and assistance of these EU-wide law enforcement and criminal justice agencies.

Cybercrime is a fast-growing transnational threat with an increasing number of criminals exploiting the speed, convenience and anonymity of the Internet to commit a diverse range of criminal activities including human trafficking. The perceived anonymity and mass audience of online transactions increase both the discretion and profitability of these services, making it very hard to identify criminals using traditional policing techniques. The use of the Internet allows the exchange of private and encrypted data, and the use of networks, newsrooms and chat rooms facilitates the grooming of victims. Dedicated websites, often on the 'dark web', organise the recruitment of victims, the marketing of the victims' services and meetings between victims and clients. Likewise, the Internet provides the medium for the production and distribution of abusive and sexually explicit material, including images of children, enables sex tourism, and allows the arranging of 'sham' marriages. Moreover, it is the Internet that acts as the platform for financial transactions and payments between those involved in human trafficking.

Human trafficking could not occur on the scale it does were it not for the complicity and collusion of corrupt officials. According to the OSCE, 'there is a strong correlation between trafficking and corruption and the trafficking of persons flourishes in part through the corruption of public officials' (2013b: 129). Corrupt officials within the wider law enforcement and criminal justice system can impact the investigation of human trafficking crimes in direct and indirect ways. Leslie Holmes argues that those subjected to human trafficking are

> victims not only of criminal gangs, but also of officials who cannot be trusted to help them counter the first form of victimisation. And if states turn a blind eye to their own officers' corrupt involvement in trafficking and/or treat trafficked persons as criminals rather than victims, there is a third form of victimisation. (2009: 85)

Corruption can obstruct investigations, prosecutions and criminal and/or civil proceedings. Corrupt officials either are directly involved in the human trafficking process or, through their omissions, enable the process to flourish. They may sell investigative information or assist traffickers in evading prosecution. They may be directly involved in trafficking individuals or related criminal activity such as prostitution or forced labour. They may also collude in the activities of organised crime by providing the traffickers with intelligence, overlooking intelligence or evidence, or providing fraudulent paperwork. Indirectly, they can also assist traffickers by, for example, not investigating cases of trafficking or obstructing efforts to effectively respond to trafficking (Holmes 2009).

Article 9 of the UNTOC's 'Measures against Corruption' states that 'in addition to the measures set forth in Article 8 of this Convention each State Party shall, to the extent appropriate and consistent with its legal system, adopt, legislative, administrative or other effective measures to promote integrity and to prevent, detect and punish the corruption of public officials'.

Prosecuting Human Trafficking

As with investigation, the prosecution of human trafficking cases poses multifaceted challenges. For Farrell, Owens and McDevitt, 'sex trafficking cases present a host of difficult problems' (2013: 24). In principle, prosecutions should be victim-centred with the human rights of the trafficked victim being the primary consideration. In this context, given the importance of victim credibility at trial, obtaining accurate and compelling evidence from victims is a prerequisite for a successful prosecution. However, as Alex Aronowitz observes, 'trafficked victims do not make good witnesses' (2017: 127).

> Due to trauma, fear, and self-blame, many change their stories or withdraw their charges. It is essential that prosecutors (and judges) understand the needs and behaviour of the victim. (Aronowitz 2017: 127)

A fundamental decision for those involved in prosecuting a potential case of trafficking is which crime to prosecute given the complexity of the relevant legislation concerning human trafficking, and then to explain the rationale for that choice to the court. Beyond that, prosecutors have a duty to ensure that the case is effectively managed, compelling evidence is presented to the court, witnesses are protected, and those witnesses who are suffering from physical or psychological problems are able to give testimony safely. Measures to protect the physical and psychological safety of victims need to be developed in collaboration with all concerned actors. The prosecution of human trafficking cases should follow uniform procedures and policies and operate to strict timelines and deadlines.

Case management is a framework which provides guidance on how cases can be managed most effectively and efficiently from pre-charge through to conclusion. It details the procedures, the roles and responsibilities of those responsible for the prosecution and the duties of the defence, and sets out the expectations of the judiciary. The process generally begins from the point when a crime is reported to law enforcement agencies. Evidence is then gathered to establish what actually happened and who was involved, and testimony is taken from witnesses to support the evidence. Case management comprises specialised processes or structures that ensure the efficient progression of cases through a judicial system and access to justice. Effective case management can help overcome obstacles to a successful prosecution. A key component of case management is cooperation between law enforcement, criminal justice and other specialised services involved in human trafficking prosecutions such as victim support agencies and case coordination mechanisms. Those involved in these highly specialised criminal cases, including police officers and prosecutors, should receive dedicated training with emphasis placed on gender-sensitivity.

Human trafficking is a gendered crime. There are gender dimensions to the supply and demand factors that underpin the crime, to the causes, to the vulnerability of victims, as well as to the gendered policy and institutional responses that seek to address human trafficking. The Trafficking Directive emphasises that men and women are trafficked for different purposes, that human trafficking is a 'gender-specific phenomenon' and that 'assistance and support measures should be gender-specific where appropriate'. Critiquing the 'limitations inherent in the criminal and economic' theoretical approaches to human trafficking, Navid Pourmokhtari recognises the emergence of 'a feminist rights-based approach (FRBA), one that views the phenomenon of human trafficking through a "gender lens"' (2015: 159). He argues that dialogue should be complemented by ways and means of empowering 'women' individually and collectively, through, for example, effective policing, legal measures designed specifically to protect their rights, and effective grass roots and community-based efforts aimed at raising awareness regarding the causes and consequences of trafficking and its implications for women. (Pourmokhtari 2015: 165)

Trafficked victims present significant challenges not only in relation to their care and protection, but as key witnesses. In some cases, victims may be unable or unwilling to testify. Indeed, 'non-cooperation and fearful behaviour of the victim can be one of the most important indicators of the possibility of a human trafficking offence' (Palmiotto 2014: 109). Non-cooperation could be because victims and/or witnesses are still under the control of, or feel threatened by, their traffickers or because of continuing psychological and/or physical harm. Trafficked victims may also have concerns about their safety and/or protection. Yet, there is a fundamental recognition on the part of those prosecuting a case that to mount a successful prosecution, the victim(s) must be seen as credible.

The interviewing of trafficked victims is a crucial part of the investigation, and those conducting interviews should respect the rights, choices and autonomy of the victim. Interviewers face layered complexities in obtaining evidence from trafficked victims. Some victims deny involvement, whilst others have impaired decision-making powers and difficulty in providing a coherent and consistent account which presents a risk of plausible invention and evidential contradiction. It is important that both the interview management and the testimony are carefully handled. Interviewing trafficked victims raises ethical questions and safety concerns. Underpinning the process should be the IOM's non-maleficence principle, 'do no harm'. Regardless of how the interview proceeds, the first concern of the interviewer should be to ensure that the conduct of the interview does not make the victims' circumstances less secure. Trafficked victims will have been exposed to risks and may still be at risk when being interviewed. The protection of victims should be the primary concern of the interviewer and principles for the protection of the victim should be followed. The prosecutor should involve the victim throughout the process, providing information on the role of the victim in the proceedings and timely and clear updates on the progress of the case.

Interviews should be conducted by interviewers specifically trained in handling human trafficking cases. Article 29 of the CoE Convention 'Specialised authorities and co-ordinating bodies' states that

> each Party shall adopt such measures as may be necessary to ensure that persons or entities are specialised in the fight against trafficking and the protection of victims. Such persons or entities shall have the necessary independence in accordance with the fundamental principles of the legal system of the Party, in order for them to be able to carry out their functions effectively and free from any undue pressure. Such persons or the staffs of such entities shall have adequate training and financial resources for their tasks.

The interviewer needs to have a detailed understanding of the specifics of each victim's case, their material circumstances and psychological well-being. This knowledge will allow the interviewer to recognise impediments to victim cooperation. Barriers to cooperation include age, gender, religious belief and cultural background. Victims do not always tell the truth and can respond to questions in a manner primarily intended to conciliate the interviewer.

The credibility of the victim as an interviewee, and as a witness in court, is key to a successful prosecution. This is influenced by intrinsic and extrinsic factors. Trauma, confusion, hostility and mistrust can affect the response of the victim to the interview process. Likewise, fear of possible consequences following the interview process, which might include reprisals against the victim or her/his family, and/or the belief that the process will lead to detention, deportation or prosecution can influence the response of the victim to questioning. Any of these factors, or a combination of them, may lead to questions not being answered truthfully or evaded.

There is also the potential for a continuing threat to the victim during the investigation and trial. The Trafficking Directive states that

> victims of trafficking who have already suffered the abuse and degrading treatment which trafficking commonly entails…should be protected from secondary victimisation and further trauma during the criminal proceedings. Unnecessary repetition of interviews during investigation, prosecution and trial should be avoided, for instance, where appropriate, through the production, as soon as possible in the proceedings, of video recordings of those interviews.

For the law enforcement or criminal justice practitioner more familiar with obtaining interview evidence through 'interrogation' techniques, 'questioning skills' and behaviours appropriate to gathering evidence from a victim need to be purposely developed including active listening and observation capabilities, empathy, patience, non-prejudice, cultural competency, composure, clarity and the maintenance of a professional and ethical demeanour throughout the interview.

When interviewing a trafficked victim, the overarching aim is to obtain an accurate account of events from the perspective of the victim. Specific techniques and good practice methodologies can help. The approach taken during the interview should reflect the particular circumstances of the case and the current disposition of the victim. To this end, a non-judgemental relationship and a rapport between interviewer and interviewee based on mutual respect facilitate a frank exchange of information. If the victim needs food, drink or medical attention, this should be supplied before the interview begins. The interviewer should introduce all those present and explain their roles and make sure that the victim understands the purpose of the interview, why she/he is being interviewed, how the interview will proceed and how long it will last. The victim should be informed that the interview is confidential, that she/he has the right to ask questions and that their consent is required for the interview to be conducted. The interview's location should be secure and private in order to reassure the victim that she/he is safe and protected. Ideally, the interviewer should be the same gender as the victim (EIGE 2018). If there is a language barrier, an approved interpreter, but not a friend or member of the victim's ethnic community, should be appointed. Likewise, the victim should be offered the support of an impartial legal representative or counsellor. The victim should be informed that the interview is confidential and their consent to being interviewed should be obtained.

The prosecution of human trafficking cases is a shifting environment that presents evolving challenges making it potentially necessary to adapt prosecutorial approaches. Victim protection should be a primary concern and no approach should be taken that could put a trafficked victim at risk. Inadequate or limited victim protection and the victims' fear of limited or no security can affect their demeanour and influence if, or how, they give evidence in court. The Group of Experts on Action Against Trafficking in Human Beings (GRETA) recognises the need to prevent intimidation of victims of trafficking before, during and after trial.

> Victims are sometimes reluctant to give statements because of threats of revenge from the perpetrators and therefore the protection of victims and witnesses of trafficking is important to reassure them to take the step of testifying. Victims also need to be prepared psychologically to give statements and NGOs providing assistance to victims have an important role to play in this regard. (GRETA 2016: 24)

GRETA cites as good practice the use of video and audio conferencing, rather than the victim appearing in court in person, and the guarantee of anonymity and the possibility of excluding the public from human trafficking trials to prevent witness intimidation.

Aside from the intrinsic problems of ensuring the physical and psychological safety of the victim and converting victim evidence into a conviction, the adoption of a victim-centred approach has been criticised for being less concerned with human rights and more a legal necessity to secure a positive verdict, especially in countries which practice the common law where intercept evidence is not always admissible. In the context of US' victim support mechanisms, Yoon Jin Shin argues that

> victim protection and support are not the rights of victims, but are predominantly measures to secure victims as healthy and stable witnesses…this victim treatment scheme is far from adopting a 'rights-based' or 'victim-centred approach as claimed by the US government'. (Shin 2017: 81)

A further concern is that by seemingly privileging the victim during the trial stage of the criminal justice process, the defendant could be denied a fair trial. Tony Ward and Shahrzad Fouladvand recognise that it is 'essential to a fair trial that the defendant must be able to adduce evidence that is of substantial probative value and raise questions that potentially afford grounds for reasonable doubt' (2018: 155). However, the potential for secondary victimisation may afford compelling grounds for limiting the defendant's 'right to confrontation' provided there are what the ECtHR calls 'sufficient counterbalancing factors' to ensure a fair trial…the weaknesses that commonly exist in the evidence of alleged trafficking victims, such as inconsistent or false previous statements and motives to present themselves as victims, will very often be ones that can be amply demonstrated to the court without needing to cross-examine the complainant. (Ward and Fouladvand 2018: 155)

Brexit and Human Trafficking

In terms of pursuing human traffickers, despite a complex regime of opt-outs, UK authorities historically have worked very closely with EU counterparts and made extensive use of a spectrum of mechanisms under EU criminal justice and law enforcement legislation. The UK has ratified the CoE Convention, and after initially opting out of the Trafficking Directive, mainly over concerns about the extension of investigations by the law enforcement agencies of member states into human trafficking cases on UK sovereign territory, it adopted the Directive in 2011. The UK has been an active, and frequently leading, participant in the gamut of EU counter-trafficking mechanisms and institutions including Europol, Eurojust, the European Arrest Warrant (EAW), Joint Investigative Teams (JITs), the European Criminal Records Information System (ECRIS), and the Schengen Second Generation Information Services (SIS II). Between 2009 and 2018, Rob Wainright, a British civil servant, was the director of Europol. It has been estimated that 40% of all intelligence collected by Europol comes from the UK, and 40% of all Europol cases have British involvement (*Guardian* 2017; *Politico* 2016).

Partnership and collaboration are indispensable prerequisites to effective investigation and prosecution of human trafficking cases. The discovery of 39 suffocated Vietnamese migrants in a refrigerated lorry in the port of Purfleet in Essex in October 2019 instigated an investigation that involved law enforcement and criminal justice agencies from Bulgaria where the lorry cab was registered, Belgium and France where the cab had travelled prior to crossing to the UK, and the Republic of Ireland where the company that owned the cab was based and where one of its drivers lived. All these states are members of the EU. Complex investigations are expedited by the mechanisms and institutions established by the EU to facilitate investigation and prosecution between member states. The loss of access to these mechanisms would seriously impede the UK's capacity to counter serious crime, including human trafficking. The UK's National Crime Agency (NCA) has stated that its priority is to ensure either continued membership of Europol or to find equivalent arrangements (Ventrella 2018: 130). Likewise, the NCA recognises that not having access to the Eurojust databases and SIS II would undermine investigations to the extent that, as a contingency, it has been surreptitiously transferring records from EU databases to the UK's National Police Computer (*Guardian*, 27 July 2019a).

It is unlikely that having left the EU the UK will have any formal influence on the EU's counter-trafficking strategy. As a third country, the UK will no longer be a member of the Europol Management Board, the body that decides the EU's strategic response to organised crime, or the Standing Committee on Operational Cooperation on Internal Security (COSI) that sets strategic priorities. At an operational level, the means and methods of delivering on the priorities are decided through the groups that comprise the European multidisciplinary platform against criminal threats (EMPACT). Prior to Brexit, the UK had a disproportionate influence on EMPACT, chairing 4 out of 13 groups, and co-chairing another 5. It has been suggested that the UK's access to high-quality intelligence, including on criminality connected with human trafficking, might be leveraged into a privileged third country relationship with Europol, although potential use of bulk interceptions post-Brexit might bring the UK into conflict with the EU's General Data Protection Regulation (GPDR).

In terms of negotiating continued relations with Eurojust, Liz Campbell argues that, 'one obstacle lies in the political acceptability of this to other member states…another obstacle lies in the fact that continued involvement will also entail oversight from the supranational EU institutions' (2017: 7). The position of the Conservative governments of Theresa May and Boris Johnson has been that after Brexit, the UK will no longer accept the jurisdiction of the Court of Justice of the European

Union (CJEU), the ultimate legal arbiter of criminal justice and security policies and measures within the EU. Unless a compromise can be found, this would, *prima facie*, preclude future UK cooperation with EU institutions or its use of EU counter-trafficking mechanisms. As the House of Lords EU Committee notes, 'Europol is accountable to the CJEU, and any operational agreement will have to take this into account' (2018: para. 97).

The EU chief negotiator, Michel Barnier, made clear in 2018 that after the Brexit transition period, Britain would no longer be able to use the EAW, the mechanism which allows for fast, simple arrest, detention and extradition of citizens of EU member states (*New European* 2018). In a paper published in February 2020, the UK government accepted that it would not seek to participate in either the EAW or Eurojust as part of its relationship with the EU following the transition period (HM Government 2020: 27). It is possible that the UK might seek to negotiate a third-country arrangement with the EU regarding surrender similar to the arrangement that exists with Iceland and Norway. However, these arrangements took eight years to negotiate. Moreover, third-country status is a long way from the UK's current leading role. The UK, historically a rule-maker rather than a rule-taker, would find itself, as one Norwegian specialist observes, 'listening in at the keyhole, rather than being a full decision-making participant in EU-related security and defence discussions' (Deighton 2019: 112). In September 2019, the British and Irish governments announced a scheme to replace the use of the EAW between the two countries post-Brexit based on the 1957 Council of Europe Convention on Extradition, whilst admitting that the new arrangement would be 'sub-optimal' and 'slower and more resource intensive' (BBC 2019). Germany, Austria and Slovenia no longer extradite their citizens to the UK even during the transition period.

The ramifications of Brexit for the UK's internal security have received less media coverage or attention from politicians than other aspects of Brexit such as economic prosperity and national sovereignty. As a member state has never withdrawn from the EU, the negotiation of a future security relationship between the UK and the EU is breaking new ground. Yet, it is concerning that with such as short transition period, there is so little clarity or detail about a future partnership. As Helena Carrapico,

Antonia Niehuss and Chloé Berthélémy observe, 'the UK is faced with having to develop new forms of cooperation with its neighbours to fight ever more transnational security threats, as well as new strategies to maintain its leading role as an international security actor' (2018: 148). Moreover, the Trafficking Directive that provides an overarching guarantee of minimum standards of support for trafficked victims will, post-Brexit, most likely not be available in UK jurisdictions, for example, under the law in England and Wales. The Anti-Trafficking Monitoring Group (ATMG), a group of nine NGOs that monitors the UK response to CoE Convention and Trafficking Directive obligations, has formulated a series of recommendations to minimise the impact of Brexit on countering human trafficking in the UK.

> The UK Government must pursue access to European criminal justice and security measures to the greatest extent possible…the UK must accept some measure of the jurisdiction of the CJEU…primary legislation must be introduced which transposes the rights of victims to support and assistance, as detailed in the Trafficking Directive, into domestic law in England and Wales…the UK Government should introduce primary legislation which transposes EU labour law that protects worker's rights… the UK Government must undertake an impact assessment for any new proposed law and policy related to immigration to assess its likely impact on efforts to tackle modern slavery. (ATG 2017: 25)

The impact of Brexit on the UK's immigration policy will also likely have an attendant effect on the prevalence of labour trafficking. In December 2018, the British government published a White Paper that sets out its proposed immigration policy after the UK leaves the EU. One of the aims of the White Paper is to respond to the concerns of business leaders that the UK's intention to end the free movement of people, one of the core freedoms enshrined in the Treaty of Rome, will lead to labour shortages. In November 2019, the UK's Office of National Statistics announced that the number of EU migrants entering the UK from EU member states in the year up to June 2019 was at its lowest level since 2003 (Guardian 2019b). A key mechanism to plug this potential labour gap whilst limiting settled migration to the UK is the Temporary Migration

Programme (TMP). In September 2018, the May government announced a pilot scheme called the Seasonal Workers Pilot (SWP) to run from March 2019 to bring in workers from outside the EU to work on UK farms on six-month visas to tackle labour shortages at peak periods in the agricultural year. The White Paper also proposes a route for short-term migrants at all skills levels to work in the UK as 'temporary short-term workers' for up to 12 months to be followed by a mandatory 12-month 'cooling-off' period during which the person cannot reapply.

TMPs have a long history in developed world countries as mechanisms that allow short-term immigration, but restrict leave to remain to a fixed term. Often the visas on which workers enter are tied to the sponsorship of a particular employer, although the government's SWP seemingly allows migrants to change employer. The non-governmental organisation Focus on Labour Exploitation (FLEX) notes that other features of TMPs include 'multiple dependencies on employers, such as the requirement to stay in employer-provided accommodation; limited or no family re-unification rights; limited or no access to benefits and public services; and no pathways to permanent residence' (2019: 16).

FLEX argues that TMPs can lead to an increased risk of labour exploitation.

> Migration policies that restrict the rights of workers will contribute to an increased risk of labour abuse and exploitation for migrant workers and may create situations in which workers have to choose whether to remain with exploitative employers or risk destitution, homelessness and deportation. (FLEX 2019: 45–46)

There is concern that TMPs might legitimise inferior working conditions analogous to the conditions imposed on persons currently victims of human trafficking for labour exploitation. Unlike the pre-Brexit right to free movement that guarantees the same rights for EU migrants as UK workers and access to UK welfare benefits, 'temporary migrants do not enjoy the same social or political rights associated with citizenship: they cannot vote, stand for election or access social benefits (FLEX 2019: 17). Ultimately, FLEX recommends that 'the [UK] Government should ensure the same rights for all migrant workers in order to prevent exploitation' (2019: 45).

In February, the recently re-elected Johnson government announced its intention to introduce a points-based system similar to that used by Australia. Under the new system, potential migrant workers will not be given a work visa if they are low skilled and/or do not speak English to a specified standard. This will particularly affect low-skilled migrant workers from EU countries who, as a consequence of the free movement of people principle within the EU, have been able to work legally in any EU member state. Barbara Drozdowicz, the chief executive of the East European Resource Centre, considers the proposed post-Brexit points-based system liable to result in more human trafficking.

> Let's not kid ourselves: someone will have to do the dirty, low-paid jobs, from construction to food processing to social care. Where are these workers going to come from? Even now, as eastern Europeans have full access to labour market, Poles and Romanians are two of five top nationalities who are reported victims of modern slavery in the UK. It is easy to imagine how increasing pressure to drive down labour costs as the supply of low-skilled workers weakens will translate into much more severe coercion and abuse. (Guardian, 20th February 2020)

Conclusion

Pursuing traffickers is not only an obligation for any political system based on justice and the rule of law, but a key element of an effective prevention strategy. The effective investigation of human trafficking crimes, the prosecution and the conviction of those involved in trafficking act as a deterrent and potentially alter the risk-reward calculation of would-be traffickers. Investigation is, however, costly in terms of both human and physical resources. Pro-active investigations, employing the ILP model, whilst the most effective response to organised human trafficking, involve teams of specialist investigators potentially supported by criminal justice personnel. Given its complexity, countering human trafficking often involves invasive SIT. These techniques, whilst the most effective way of gathering evidence, need expert oversight, especially in common law jurisdictions, to ensure that the evidence gathered will be admissible in any subsequent criminal trial. For this reason, as well as the productivity benefits of a joined-up counter-trafficking response, the pursuit of traffickers requires close collaboration and overlap between investigators and prosecutors.

As in other areas of organised criminal activity, financial investigation can be used to gather evidence—following the money—but FI can also lead to the seizure of the proceeds of crime and potentially the payment of restitution to victims. Forensic accountancy adds a further layer of expertise to investigations. Although asset seizing has the potential to increase the risk and potentially diminish the rewards for traffickers, arguably the fragmented and often small-scale nature of much human trafficking makes financial investigation a less viable counter-crime tactic than in other areas of organised crime.

The international legal framework, including the Trafficking Protocol, the CoE Convention and the Trafficking Directive, officially puts the victim at the centre of the prosecutorial process. Successful prosecution of victims therefore requires sensitive, but effective, case management. Inherently vulnerable, victims' physical and psychological well-being needs ensuring, whilst they also need protection from reprisals from their trafficker, and/or shielding from the threat of re-trafficking. Whilst protection is a human rights imperative, victim testimony is often a crucial element of a prosecution, hence criticism that victim protection is less concerned with rights and more concerned with obtaining a conviction. The challenges presented by the centrality of the victim to the prosecution of human trafficking cases have led to calls for an increase in the use of SIT to obtain compelling evidence removing the need to rely on victim testimony. The technical requirements and cost of SIT, however, currently restrict its use to developed world states, and the standard of evidence gathered often fails to reach the threshold required to achieve a conviction.

The withdrawal of the UK from the EU at the end of January 2020 is likely to prove a further setback for the construction of a holistic response to the pursuit of traffickers, primarily in the UK and the EU. However, Brexit is also a retrogressive step in the global push to construct a universal approach to countering the threat. The UK has played a leading role in the development and management of the EU's sophisticated law enforcement and criminal justice mechanisms and institutions. Prior to Brexit, a disproportionate amount of criminal intelligence circulated between EU member states regarding transnational organised crime was provided by the UK agencies, and the UK chaired or co-chaired more EMPACT groups than other member states. Whilst UK law enforcement and criminal justice agencies have indicated they want third-party involvement in EU mechanisms such as JITs, the EAW, ECRIS and SIS II, there is no certainty that this will be negotiable by the end of the transition period in December 2020.

References

Anti-Trafficking Monitoring Group (2017), 'Brexit and the UK's fight against modern slavery', July. Available at https://www.antislavery.org/wp-content/uploads/2017/07/ATMG-Brexit-paper.pdf.

Aronowitz, A. (2017), *Human Trafficking*. Santa Barbara: ABC-CLIO.

British Broadcasting Corporation (2019), 'Brexit: Governments agree plans to replace European Arrest Warrant', September. Available at https://www.bbc.co.uk/news/uk-northern-ireland-49576159.

Campbell, L. (2017), 'Beyond Brexit – Beyond Borders Mutual Assistance in Policing and Investigating Organised Crime', Durham University Centre for Criminal Law and Criminal Justice Discussion Paper, May. Available at http://borderpeople.info/site/wp-content/uploads/BrexitExecutiveSummary.pdf.

Carrapico, H., Niehuss, A. & Berthélémy, C. (2018), *Brexit and Internal Security: Political and Legal Concerns on the Future UK-EU Relationship*. London: Palgrave Macmillan.

Deighton, A. (2019), 'Brexit Diplomacy: the Strange Case of Security and Defence', *Diplomatica*, Vol. 1, No. 1.

European Institute for Gender Equality (2018), *Gender-specific measures in anti-trafficking actions*. Luxembourg: EU Publications Office.

Farrell, A., Bouché, V., and Wolfe, D. (2019), 'Assessing the Impact of State Human Trafficking Legislation on Criminal Justice System Outcomes', *Law and Policy*, Vol. 42, No. 2.

Farrell, A., Owens, C., and McDevitt, J. (2013), 'New laws but few cases: understanding the challenges to the investigation and prosecution of human trafficking cases', *Crime, Law and Social Change*, Vol. 61, No. 2.

Farrell, A., and Pfeffer, R. (2014), 'Policing Human Trafficking: Cultural Blinders and Organizational Barriers', *Annals of the American Academy*, Vol. 653, May.

Focus on Labour Exploitation (2019), *The Risks of Exploitation in Temporary Migration Programmes: A FLEX Response to the 2018 Immigration White Paper.* Available at https://www.labourexploitation.org/sites/default/files/publications/Report_Risks%20of%20Exploitation%20in%20TMPs_May%202019_Final.pdf.

Gallagher, A., and Holmes, P. (2008), 'Developing an Effective Criminal Justice Response to Human Trafficking', *International Criminal Justice Review*, Vol. 18 No. 3.

Group of Experts on Action against Trafficking in Human Beings (2016), *Compendium of good practices on the implementation of the Council of Europe Convention on Action against Trafficking in Human Beings.* Strasbourg: GRETA/Council of Europe.

Guardian (2017), 'Using security as Brexit bargaining chip is reckless and lacks credibility'. Available at https://www.theguardian.com/politics/2017/mar/30/using-security-as-brexit-bargaining-chip-is-reckless-and-lacks-credibility.

Guardian (2019a), Brexit: key strands of British policing 'in jeopardy' because of no-deal risk'. Available at https://www.theguardian.com/uk-news/2019/jul/27/nca-harvesting-eu-databases-owing-to-risk-of-no-deal-brexit.

Guardian (2019b), 'Net migration at lowest level since 2003, ONS says'. Available at https://www.theguardian.com/world/2019/nov/28/net-migration-from-eu-atlowest-level-since-2003-ons-figures-show.

Guardian (2020), 'Immigration rules post-Brexit could fuel modern slavery, say charities'. Available at https://www.theguardian.com/uk-news/2020/feb/21/immigration-rules-post-brexit-could-fuel-modern-slavery-say-charities.

Her Majesty's Government (2020), 'The Future Relationship with the EU: The UK's Approach to Negotiations', February. Available at https://assets.publishing.service.gov.uk/government/uploads/system/uploads/attachment_data/file/868874/The_Future_Relationship_with_the_EU.pdf.

Holmes, L. (2009), 'Human Trafficking & Corruption: Triple Victimisation?' in Friesendorf, C. (ed.), *Strategies Against Human Trafficking: The Role of the Security Sector*, Vienna and Geneva: National Defence Academy and Austrian Ministry of Defence and Sports.

House of Lords European Union Committee (2018), 'Brexit: the proposed UK-EU security treaty', 18th Report of Session 2017-19, July 2018. Available at https://publications.parliament.uk/pa/ld201719/ldselect/ldeucom/164/16402.htm.

International Labour Organisation (2014), *Profits and Poverty: The Economics of Forced Labour*. Geneva: ILO.

Messer, K. (2019), 'Financial Investigations: Combating Human Trafficking', *Anti-Money Laundering White Paper*, May. Available at http://files.acams.org/pdfs/2019/Karen-Messer-White-Paper.pdf?_ga=2. 189475752.2081021004.1565346569-955199830.1565346569

Middleton, B., Antonopoulos G., Papanicolaou, G. (2019), 'The Financial Investigation of Human Trafficking in the UK: Legal and Practical Perspectives', *Journal of Criminal Law*, Vol. 83, No. 4.

New European (2018), 'Barnier: UK red lines mean no European Arrest Warrant'. Available at https://www.theneweuropean.co.uk/top-stories/ michel-barnier-uk-red-lines-no-european-arrest-warrant-1-5567376.

Organization for Security and Cooperation in Europe (2013b), 'OSCE Resource Police Training Guide: Trafficking in Human Beings', SPMU Publication Series, Vol. 10.

Palmiotto, M. (2014), *Combating Human Trafficking: A Multidisciplinary Approach*. Boca Ratan: CRC Press.

Politico (2016), 'Europol first in line for life after Brexit'. Available at https:// www.politico.eu/article/europol-first-in-line-for-life-after-brexitvb-law-enforcement-rob-wainwright.

Pourmokhtari, N. (2015), 'Global Human Trafficking Unmasked', *Journal of Human Trafficking*, Vol. 1, No. 2.

Ratcliffe, J. (2008), 'Intelligence-Led Policing' in Wortley, R., Mazerolle, L., and Rombouts, S., *Environmental Criminology and Crime Analysis* (ed.). Cullompton: Willan.

Shin, Y. J. (2017), *A Transnational Human Rights Approach to Human Trafficking: Empowering the Powerless*. Leiden: Brill.

United Nations Office on Drugs and Crime (2014a), *SOP Manual for Law Enforcement Personnel of the Central Asia countries on the cases related to human trafficking and smuggling of migrants*. Vienna: UNODC.

United Nations Office on Drugs and Crime (2014b), *Global report on trafficking in persons*. Vienna: UNODC. Available at https://www.unodc.org/docu-ments/data-and-analysis/glotip/GLOTIP_2014_full_report.pdf.

Ventrella, M. (2018), 'Brexit and the Fight Against Human Trafficking: Actual Situation and Future Uncertainty', *Marmara Journal of European Studies*, Vol. 26, No.1.

Ward, T., and Fouladvand, S. (2018), 'Human Trafficking, Victims' Rights and Fair Trials', *Journal of Criminal Law*, Vol. 82, No. 2.

4

Protecting the Victims

Abstract The damage caused to the physical and psychological health of trafficked victims has been described as a global health concern. Exacerbating this harm, victims are also often prosecuted for crimes, such as prostitution and drug dealing, committed as a result of their exploitation. Non-punishment provisions in international law are not uniformly understood or consistently applied. Moreover, victim rights such as privacy, confidentiality, protection of their identity and data, and access to legal services are frequently not protected. There is evidence that the provision of these rights remains inconsistent and sporadic. In particular, this inconsistency is apparent in the uneven effectiveness across national jurisdictions of national referral mechanisms, intended to provide the vital roles of identifying, protecting and assisting victims of trafficking.

Keywords: Victim health • Non-punishment • Victim rights • National referral mechanisms

The protection of victims and victim rights lies at the heart of the Trafficking Protocol, CoE Convention and Trafficking Directive. Over the past decade, a general agreement has emerged within the international

© The Author(s) 2020
S. Massey, G. Rankin, *Exploiting People for Profit*,
https://doi.org/10.1057/978-1-137-43413-5_4

community that trafficking itself is a serious violation of human rights. For example, both the CoE Convention and the Trafficking Directive identify trafficking as a violation of human rights. The UN General Assembly and the Human Rights Council (HRC) have repeatedly affirmed that trafficking violates and impairs fundamental human rights, as have many international human rights mechanisms. This lead has been taken up by states, many of which have developed a victim-centred response to human trafficking within their territories. However, in practice, the record of the victim-centred approach, in terms of not only human rights but also law enforcement and criminal justice outcomes, is equivocal.

The chapter firstly assesses the effects of trafficking on victims in terms of physical and psychological trauma, as well as the criminalisation of victims for offences committed whilst in a trafficking situation. It continues by setting out the rights that victims should be able to exercise in international law. Victims are entitled to be treated with fairness and dignity, to be offered and receive information, protection, assistance, compensation and restitution. Yet, although mechanisms are in place for victim protection, these are frequently criticised by victim support groups. The chapter reviews protective measures available to victims, and potential victims, throughout the trafficking process, whilst assessing where responsibility lies for providing protection. It concludes with a critical examination of national referral mechanisms questioning the extent of the protection that these key mechanisms deliver.

The Impact of Human Trafficking on Victims

Human trafficking can have serious physical and psychological effects on victims. A study by Sian Oram et al. of female and male trafficking survivors in England and Wales found that 'many survivors experience medium to long-term physical, sexual, and mental health problems, including injuries, sexually transmitted infections (STIs), and probable depression, anxiety, and post-traumatic stress disorder (PTSD)' (Oram et al. 2016: 1076). Victims can receive traumatic physical injuries, contract diseases such as HIV/Aids and STIs and suffer psychological damage. Physical and mental violence can occur both prior to trafficking and whilst in the

Box 4.1 Health risks before and during the human trafficking process

Overall, 42.3% of men and 76.5% of women reported physical violence during trafficking. Injuries were sustained by 32.7% of men and 67.4% of women as a result of either violence or occupational accidents; 21.2% of men and 23.5% of women reported that these injuries caused ongoing pain or difficulty.

Two thirds of women reported being forced to have sex during trafficking, including 95% of women trafficked for sexual exploitation, 54% trafficked for domestic servitude, and 21% trafficked for other forms of labour exploitation.

The prevalence of pre-trafficking violence was also high. In total, 28.9% of men and 58.2% of women reported pre-trafficking physical violence. In addition, 30% of women reported pre-trafficking sexual violence, perpetrated predominantly by partners (9.2%) and family members (5.1%).

Source: Oram, S. et al. (2016), 'Human Trafficking and Health: A Survey of Male and Female Survivors in England', American Journal of Public Health, Vol. 106, No. 6

trafficking situation. Victims endure very different experiences. Some are held captive and relentlessly assaulted, while others are not abused physically, but are psychologically tormented and live in fear of harm to themselves or their family members. The research by Oram et al. collated the prevalence of health risks before and after trafficking (see Box 4.1).

The violence that trafficked victims suffer can be physical and/or sexual, and includes restrictions on their movement, as well as threats to their family and/or children. Physical violence can include assaults and being threatened or injured by weapons. Sexual violence includes victims being forced or intimidated into performing sexual acts against their will. The impact of this violence can result in a wide range of chronic health problems from fatigue and weight loss to neurological symptoms, as well as potential mental health issues. It can also result in victims becoming withdrawn, further enhancing their isolation and potentially making them more dependent on their traffickers. Oram et al.'s study also found that 'seventy-one percent of the participants reported that they remained afraid of the traffickers even after they were out of the trafficking situation' (2016: 1075).

Trafficked victims can suffer from adverse sexual and reproductive health complications, typically as a result of sexual violence and coercion experienced during the trafficking situation. This can include the risk of acquiring a range of STIs and/or HIV/AIDS through their engagement in commercial sex, sexual violence, experiences of coerced sex and unsafe sex.

Psychological symptoms can manifest themselves as mental health issues including depression, anxiety, hostility and PTSD, as well as the effects of emotional abuse. The impact of trauma can include dissociation and depersonalisation, an altered sense of time, memory impairment, acute indifference and apathy, the fragmentation of perception, feeling, consciousness and memory and flashbacks. The essence of trauma is that it overwhelms the victim's psychological and biological coping mechanisms. This occurs when internal and external resources are inadequate to cope with the external threat. Depressive symptoms can include feeling very sad, worthless and a feeling of hopelessness about the future. The symptoms of hostility can include feeling annoyed or easily irritated, having temper outbursts and becoming easily upset. Trafficked victims have also been diagnosed with PTSD, an anxiety disorder caused by very stressful, frightening or distressing events, which may be recurring. PTSD can manifest itself through re-experiencing traumatic events which can comprise recurrent thoughts or memories of terrifying events, recurring nightmares or sudden emotional or physical reactions when reminded of a traumatic event. The disorder can also lead to agitation, insomnia, difficulty in concentrating, feeling irritable and outbursts of anger. Victims suffering from PTSD can also feel numb, detached, lack emotion and lack belief that they do not have a future.

The prevalence and the severity of ill-health-related symptoms of human trafficking have led Cathy Zimmerman and Ligia Kiss to advocate it being designated a 'global health concern' (2017). The ILO's estimate of 40.3 million human trafficking victims significantly outnumbers the 30.5 million people suffering from HIV/AIDS (ILO 2017). Zimmerman and Kiss argue that in terms of harm, 'most trafficked people experience violence and hazardous, exhausting work, and few emerge without longer-term, sometimes disabling, physical and psychological damage' (2017: 8).

There can be several stages of recovery including hostility, loss of orientation, reconstruction and remembering prior to social reintegration. Victims can adopt a number of survival strategies typical of coercive relationships in response to systematic abuse. The three key survival strategies are avoidance, identifying with the trafficker known as Stockholm syndrome, and numbing. A study of women victims of trafficking in Ghana found that there is a connection between social reintegration and community support reinforcing other studies that demonstrate 'the importance of social support in mitigating PTSD' (Okech et al. 2018: 215).

The shock of the trafficking situation can affect the trafficked victim's emotional and intellectual capacity which can impair his/her ability to engage effectively with legal proceedings. It may result in victims being unable to provide testimony or influence their credibility or reliability as witnesses. The impact of trafficking on the health of victims can also cause impaired cognitive functioning which can equally affect how trafficked victims provide detailed evidence related to the crime or make decisions about cooperating in a prosecution.

Victims of human trafficking are often compelled to commit criminal offences by their traffickers. Shahrzad Fouladvand and Tony Ward argue that, rather than being passive victims, individuals who approach people smugglers to transport them abroad, possibly intending to work as prostitutes, are engaging in a form of 'resilience, a way of seeking control over one's life and escaping from extreme poverty, gender-based violence and other hardships' (2019: 52). However,

> when the smugglers turn out to be traffickers, the migrant may be faced with such levels of coercion and manipulation that they lose any meaningful degree of autonomy. Such cases raise a thorny question in the theory and doctrine of criminal law: the extent to which people can be held responsible for bringing about their own lack of responsibility. (Fouladvand and Ward 2019: 52)

Article 26 of the CoE, known as the 'non-punishment provision', states that 'each Party shall, in accordance with the basic principles of its legal system, provide for the possibility of not imposing penalties on victims for their involvement in unlawful activities, to the extent that they have been compelled to do so'. The principle of non-punishment of victims is affirmed in a number of international legal instruments. Whilst the Trafficking Protocol does not contain any explicit provision concerning the non-punishment of victims, it is explicit in the CoE Convention and the Trafficking Directive. To comply with international standards, states are obliged to provide a 'non-punishment of women and adolescents trafficked in Europe' provision in their national law. The Recital to the Trafficking Directive states that

> victims of trafficking in human beings should, in accordance with the basic principles of the legal systems of the relevant Member States, be protected from prosecution or punishment for criminal activities such as the use of false documents, or offences under legislation on prostitution or immigration, that they have been compelled to commit as a direct consequence of being subject to trafficking. The aim of such protection is to safeguard the human rights of victims, to avoid further victimisation and to encourage them to act as witnesses in criminal proceedings against the perpetrators.

In the context of prosecuting human trafficking crimes, the OSCE contends that

> victims of trafficking are also witnesses of serious crime. The non-punishment provision will, if applied correctly, equally and fairly, enable States to improve their prosecution rates whilst ensuring critical respect for the dignity and safety of all victims of trafficking who, but for their trafficked status, would not have committed the offence at all. (OSCE 2013a: 32)

Yet, there is significant evidence that the application of the 'non-punishment provision' varies within and across jurisdictions. Julia Maria Muraszkiewicz argues that whether the provision applies to particular victims

> may not necessarily depend on whether they have been compelled to commit a crime as a result of their trafficking situation, but instead depends on the factors of victimhood that are recognised by society and relevant stakeholders (e.g. police, lawyers, judges). These factors include gender, their personal circumstances, migration status, proximity to the criminal world etc. (2019: 203)

This conclusion is borne out by research undertaken by Carolina Villacampa and Núria Torres into the use of the provision in cases of trafficking for criminal exploitation, specifically prostitution, in Spain. The study finds a 'lack of knowledge by some criminal justice professionals of the internationally recognised non-punishment principle itself and its implementation in [Spanish] domestic law, despite the fact that it was precisely these people who should call for its application' (Villacampo and Torres 2019: 16). The findings indicate that, at least in Spain,

> both the widespread unawareness of the principle's validity and the scant acceptance of its applicability confirm that victims of trafficking for criminal exploitation are essentially treated as offenders as they make their way through the criminal justice system, as they are unlikely to be exempted of criminal liability for the crimes they have been forced to commit. (Villacampo and Torres 2019: 16)

Victim Rights

Victims who agree to assist with an investigation or testify in criminal proceedings are entitled to be treated fairly, professionally, and with dignity and respect, be kept informed and given relevant information, apply for compensation or restitution, and have information about them treated with privacy and confidentiality. They are equally entitled to confidentiality and privacy during criminal investigations and proceedings. Article 6 of the Trafficking Protocol states that 'in appropriate cases and to the extent possible under domestic law, each State Party shall protect the privacy and identity of victims of human trafficking, including, inter alia, by making legal proceedings relating to such trafficking confidential'. Confidentiality should include measures to ensure that victims are not named to their family and friends and that any correspondence, from any agency, is not sent directly to an address that could lead to their identification. Trafficked victims should not be named, whenever legally possible, within court proceedings or reports in the media. Also, again subject to legal considerations, what victims say in judicial proceedings should not be repeated. Confidentiality is applicable during court proceedings and the identity of trafficked persons should be protected. Any data or information about a trafficked victim who is to testify should not be made available to any person, including the victim's family, without the consent of the trafficked victim.

These confidentiality principles are also applicable to all agencies involved in the NRM process. All communications with trafficked victims should remain confidential and any data should be handled securely. Agencies with responsibilities towards the trafficked victims should ensure that they are fully informed as to the purpose of the collection of data about them and the uses to which it will be put, as well as to their own rights to access the data. They should also ensure that no personal data is released unless the victim gives written and fully informed consent authorising the release of personal data for specific purposes and uses (IOM 2007).

Article 6.3 of the Trafficking Protocol states that

> each State Party shall consider implementing measures to provide for the physical, psychological and social recovery of victims of human trafficking, including, in appropriate cases, in cooperation with non-governmental organisations, other relevant organisations and other elements of civil society, and, in particular, the provision of counselling and information, in particular as regards their legal rights, in a language that the victim of human trafficking understands.

Trafficked victims should have the right to legal services including information about their rights, legal remedies and the options available to them. This legal assistance can be provided by independent lawyers from NGOs, civil society or the private sector. Legal assistance gives trafficked victims access to justice to ensure that victims are aware of their rights and understand them both linguistically and legally, are able to provide additional information and are able to participate in proceedings.

Victims also have the right to compensation defined as a payment for any personal injury, loss or damage resulting from a criminal offence and a means of redressing the rights violations experienced by trafficked victims. There is a right under the CoE Convention to claim compensation under international legal instruments and it can be claimed from either the trafficker or the State. Article 17 of the Trafficking Directive requires that victims of human trafficking have access to existing compensation schemes available to other victims of violent crimes. The EU Victims Directive also provides for the right of victims to obtain a decision on compensation in the course of criminal proceedings. Compensation can be claimed in criminal and/or civil proceedings. In a majority of States Parties to the CoE Convention, civil claims can also be made through criminal proceedings. Trafficked victims should be entitled to legal assistance when making a claim for compensation. On the occasion of the 2019 European Anti-trafficking Day, Secretary-General of the Council of Europe, Marija Pejčinović Burić, announced that 'justice must also be done to the victims of trafficking—by making sure they receive compensation, they are protected from being trafficked again and they are given sufficient help to put their lives back together' (Council of Europe 2019). However, GRETA contends that, in practice, it is still very rare for victims of trafficking to obtain compensation from their traffickers or from the state, declaring that the monitoring of compensation mechanisms put in place by States Parties will be one of its priorities in the next reporting period (Council of Europe 2019).

In the UK context, there has been criticism of the obstacles placed in the way of victims claiming compensation. FLEX highlights the absence in the Modern Slavery Act (2015) of a specific civil remedy for human trafficking and modern slavery. This is apparently in breach of the UK's international and European legal obligations. FLEX describes some of the impediments to victims claiming compensation in the UK.

> Language barriers, fear, mental health issues and a range of other vulnerabilities mean that victims often need help to navigate the legal process, from completing forms and making a written application, to responding to official letters or speaking with solicitors. However, the support available through the UK's NRM is limited, as support workers are not funded to attend legal meetings or provide other legal assistance. 39 Support providers also report limited knowledge of the legal avenues available to victims, and rarely inform victims of their rights to compensation. (2016: 11)

Victim Protection

International law, at least ostensibly, prioritises victim protection and assistance as a primary consideration in all human trafficking cases. Assistance should be available to potential victims of all forms of exploitation that result from being trafficked in accordance with the inclusive definition of a victim in Article 4(a) of the CoE Convention: 'victim shall mean any natural person who is subject to trafficking in human beings as defined in this article'. In practice, a victim-centred approach focuses on developing a relationship of trust with potential victims of trafficking, referring them to the appropriate services and providing information about their rights. Each potential victim should be 'provided with full information about their case, rights and possible next steps' (UNODC 2014: 71).

Article 2(b) of the Trafficking Protocol states that one of its purposes is 'to protect and assist the victims of such trafficking, with full respect for their human rights'. This is further supported by Article 6 which sets out the responsibilities for the 'assistance to and protection of victims of trafficking in persons'. The importance of victim assistance is further reinforced by the CoE Convention and the Trafficking Directive. Both these international legal instruments augment the commitment to combat human trafficking by providing mandatory provision to protect the human rights of victims. These mandatory provisions apply to victims who have been trafficked transnationally and within the borders of a sovereign state.

Article 1(b) of the CoE Convention sets out a core function

> to protect the human rights of the victims of trafficking, design a comprehensive framework for the protection and assistance of victims and witnesses, while guaranteeing gender equality, as well as to ensure effective investigation and prosecution.

According to the UNODC's standard operating procedures aimed at law enforcement personnel dealing with human trafficking cases, victims are entitled to have their human rights respected. They should be provided with protection, safety and individualised care with the right to self-determination. They should also be given full and accurate information about their treatment and its consequences, their full and informed consent should be obtained, they shouldn't be discriminated against, and their right to confidentiality should be respected. The protection of victims is always a priority and, prior to pursuing a criminal investigation, law enforcement 'must ensure victims are removed from a position of vulnerability and secured under protective custody' (UNODC 2014: 71). Victims need protection to safeguard their social, medical, physical, psychological and legal needs to assist and expedite their recovery. At all stages, the victim should be empowered. Initially, victims' immediate hygiene needs should be met including supplying clothing, food and toiletries. They should be given emotional and physical support, if required, and be kept continually informed about their situation and what will happen to them.

In order to ensure the victim's needs are being met, a needs assessment should be conducted. This entails three levels of appraisal beginning with basic needs, followed by assistance and services, and finally the needs associated with implementing the victims' rights (UNODC 2014: 71–72). Victim protection should be provided as soon as a victim of trafficking is identified and irrespective of whether a victim assists in the criminal investigation or prosecution. However, those victims that do assist in the criminal investigation or prosecution should be provided with additional protection throughout, and after, any criminal trial.

Under the CoE Convention, states have a responsibility to protect and assist trafficked victims. ICAT acknowledges that the Trafficking Protocol is 'not a particularly strong protection tool'.

> However, it does not stand alone but alongside other international legal instruments that offer stronger protection to victims of trafficking based on rights that are 'derive[d] from the inherent dignity of the human person'… as is highlighted by Principle 2 of the High Commissioner for Human Rights' Recommended Principles and Guidelines on Human Rights and Human Trafficking: 'States have a responsibility under international law to act with due diligence to…assist and protect trafficked persons'. (ICAT 2012: 6)

When a victim agrees to provide evidence in criminal proceedings, they are entitled to protection from the inception of the proceedings, as well as after they have concluded. The CoE Convention and the

Trafficking Directive underscore the obligation of states to protect victims and one of the three key priorities of the EU response following the conclusion of the EU Strategy remains to 'provide better access to and realise the rights for victims' (EU Commission 2017: 4). Witness protection measures should be used during criminal investigation and proceedings to ensure victims' human rights are protected, their safety assured and to prevent re-traumatisation. It is also highly likely that any investigation will be more successful if a victim is afforded protection measures as they will be less likely to withdraw their complaint and more likely to provide sound witness testimony. Effective protection measures can minimise any threats to victims and their families during the criminal investigation and proceedings, but especially during the court proceedings when both the victim and the perpetrator are in the court at the same time.

The European Commission has made support for victims of crime a priority and is taking steps to ensure that their needs are met. Appropriate treatment is seen as a demonstration of society's solidarity with each individual victim and recognition that such treatment is essential to the moral integrity of society. It is therefore crucial not only to combat and prevent crime, but also to properly support and protect individuals who do fall victim to crime. The EU action to address these needs, the Council Framework Decision on the standing of victims in criminal proceedings, established basic rights for victims of crime within the EU. This was replaced by Directive 2012/29/EU, sometimes called the Victims Directive, that entered into force in November 2012 and which establishes minimum standards for the rights, support and protection of victims of crime. This includes minimum standards on the rights to access information, support, protection and basic procedural rights in criminal proceedings, as well as containing more concrete and comprehensive rights for victims and clearer obligations for member states.

The protection measures incorporated in the Victims Directive are targeted at different stages of the criminal proceedings. Before the trial, once a victim has agreed to participate in an investigation and subsequent court proceedings, it is essential to consider both their safety and how to effectively remove some of their fears regarding giving evidence. Victims who are not in protective custody or being sheltered in 'safe housing' under an NRM may need other protection measures. These can include a direct telephone link or a panic button that connected to a law enforcement agency. Prior to going to court, consideration should be given to the testimony options of the victim. In some instances, victims who are not nationals of that state have been allowed to return to their home state. They then either give evidence by video or an officer from a law enforcement agency travels to the victim's state and takes evidence either on a voluntary basis or by applying for MLA. Further testimony options include victims giving a video-recorded interview which can be admitted by the court as the witness's evidence. In England and Wales, video recordings of interviews of adult complainants in sexual offence trials will automatically be admissible in court proceedings, upon application, unless this is contrary to the interests of justice or would dilute the quality of the complainant's evidence. Trafficked victims who are giving evidence in person in court proceedings can be taken for pre-court visits enabling them to become habituated with the court environment. Victims can also be supported by NGOs before and during court proceedings.

Victims of trafficking can be given a number of options regarding how they give testimony including giving evidence in court behind screens. Victims who have returned to their home states are able to give evidence via video-link. Wherever possible, trafficked victims should be accommodated in a separate waiting area and seated in court away from the defendant's family. If there is no separate area, the court should make other arrangements to keep victims safe. At the conclusion of court proceedings, the responsibility to protect the victim remains. There are ongoing responsibilities towards victims, and continued protection measures may still be required. Victims may continue to be at risk from members of the perpetrator's family or the perpetrator if acquitted. The risk may continue until they are either reintegrated, which may include medical, financial and/or legal assistance, or repatriated.

Witness protection is the means of providing protection measures for victims involved in the criminal investigation and proceedings who find themselves at risk of serious personal harm as a result of that involvement. Witness protection is generally directed to those victims who have provided crucial evidence and against whom there is a substantial threat. The openness of judicial proceedings is a fundamental principle enshrined in Article 6(1) of the European Convention on Human Rights. This principle can sometimes act as a barrier to successful prosecutions and the victims may fear that if their identity is revealed then they or their friends and family will be at risk of serious harm.

Article 12.3 of the Trafficking Directive states that

> Member States shall ensure that victims of trafficking in human beings receive appropriate protection on the basis of an individual risk assessment, inter alia, by having access to witness protection programmes and other similar measures, if appropriate and in accordance with the grounds defined any national law or procedures.

Human trafficking is often controlled by international organised criminal networks and the potential level of risk to which victims of trafficking and service delivery personnel who interact with trafficking victims are exposed should be assumed to be significant. Without overstating the degree of risk, the key to managing such situations lies in the careful assessment of the security risk involved in each case, and the constant adherence to basic best practice security procedures (IOM 2007).

In 2007, the IOM issued a handbook outlining guidelines applicable to the provision of direct assistance to victims of human trafficking relevant to the case management of human trafficking crimes. In the identification phase of the process, these guidelines include the proviso to 'do no harm' based on the first principle of medical ethics, warning that given the fragility of the victims and the trauma induced by the methods used by traffickers, 'this basic rule cannot be overstated' (IOM 2007: x). Victims should not be interviewed or examined if this 'will cause the individual to be worse off than before' (IOM 2007: x). Secondly, those involved in the identification process should 'recognise and respect the individuality of victims and, to the extent possible, provide personalized care and assistance' (IOM 2007: x). Thirdly, throughout the identification process, those involved in screening should 'recognise the right and need of victims to make their own choices and decisions, and encourage them to participate in decision-making as much as possible' (IOM 2007: x–xi). Fourthly, 'staff must provide the best possible assistance to victims of trafficking without discrimination, for example, on the basis of gender, age, disability, colour, social class, race, religion, language, political beliefs or status' (IOM 2007: xi). Finally, 'confidential trafficking data should not be disclosed without the victim's prior knowledge and informed written consent' (IOM 2007: x–xi).

In the UK context, the protection of victims has long been criticised by non-governmental organisations and civil society. In 2002, Anti-Slavery International conducted research into victim protection measures across ten countries. The fundamental finding was that 'law enforcement agencies cannot fight trafficking effectively by simply moving trafficked persons from one system of control into another—that is, from being controlled by traffickers to being controlled by law enforcement officials' (Pearson 2002: 34). In March 2018, the modern slavery charity Hestia submitted a 'super-complaint', a new system that allows designated civic organisations to raise issues about harmful patterns of policing, to Her Majesty's Inspectorate of Constabulary and Fire and Rescue Services (HMICFRS). Hestia claimed that its evidence indicated that police failings when interviewing victims were seriously hindering the successful prosecution of modern slavery cases. Hestia found that

> key themes of practice which resulted in a negative experience by victims included: victims feeling like they were not believed by the police officers who took their statements or being treated as criminals; officers prioritising pursuing immigration offences over protecting victims; female victims of sexual exploitation being interviewed by male officers using male interpreters; and victims not being informed by the police that they had decided to drop the investigation into their exploiters and traffickers. (Hestia 2019: 4)

Hestia's report into policing practice cited the experience of a Nigerian victim of sex trafficking when she sought to report the crime to a male police officer.

> He questioned everything I told him […] He even questioned why I spoke English. […]He then started searching me. He emptied my bag and took out every item. He made me empty out my pockets and take off my shoes. It was so traumatising I cannot remember it all. He said he'd throw me out if I didn't tell the truth. He shouted at me to speak up. When I asked him

to slow down because I didn't understand him, he accused me of insulting him. [...] I didn't want to complain after that, I didn't want anything to do with the police. That's why I didn't report my case. (Hestia 2019: 10)

The HMICFRS have yet to publish its response to the super-complaint. However, Hestia's research indicates that there is a serious lack of training for police officers regarding the interviewing of victims of slavery/trafficking. Of 29 police forces that responded to a freedom of information request, only two included training on modern slavery as part of their continuous development.

Victims of human trafficking are entitled to have their human rights respected and to be given protection and safety. One of the priorities of the EU Strategy has been identifying, protecting and assisting victims of trafficking. Those tasked with assisting victims should address the 'five broad needs of a victim': respect and recognition, assistance, protection, access to justice and compensation (EU Commission 2012: 6). Trafficked victims must not be subject to discriminatory treatment. All measures must be applied without discrimination, particularly, with respect to gender, ethnicity, social status, immigration status and/or the fact that a trafficked person has been trafficked previously or has participated in the sex industry or illicit activities (UNODC 2014: 71).

National Referral Mechanisms

The OSCE defines an NRM as 'a co-operative framework to allow states to identify protect and promote the human rights of trafficked persons in co-ordination with civil society' (OSCE 2014: 15). An NRM is a framework for identifying victims of human trafficking and ensuring they receive the appropriate protection and support. There are challenges for prosecutors in building and prosecuting human trafficking cases and also challenges during court proceedings to ensure the safety of victims. Protection measures can increase the number of victims who are willing to provide testimony and reduce the re-traumatisation of trafficked victims.

The scope of protective support is outlined in Article 12 of the CoE Convention.

1. Each Party shall adopt such legislative or other measures as may be necessary to assist victims in their physical, psychological and social recovery. Such assistance shall include at least:
   a. standards of living capable of ensuring their subsistence, through such measures as appropriate and secure accommodation, psychological and material assistance;
   b. access to emergency medical treatment;
   c. translation and interpretation services, when appropriate;
   d. counselling and information, in particular as regards their legal rights and the services available to them, in a language that they can understand;
   e. assistance to enable their rights and interests to be presented and considered at appropriate stages of criminal proceedings against offenders;
   f. access to education for children.

Once identified, potential victims of trafficking should be referred to victim support services. Referrals should be made following the victim's informed consent and based on their needs. Addressing victims' needs requires cooperation between different anti-trafficking actors including law enforcement, social welfare services and NGOs. The Trafficking Protocol and the CoE Convention emphasise that assistance, protection and support should be provided by the state, but in close cooperation with NGOs and civil society (Simeunovic-Patic and Copic 2010).

Competent authorities are nominated groups of people who are trained and qualified to identify trafficked victims and who should work with relevant support agencies. These competent authorities will make a judgment as to whether there are reasonable grounds to believe someone is a victim of trafficking in accord with Article 10.2 of the CoE Convention. If this decision is affirmative, a trafficked victim should not be deported and will be entitled to a 'recovery and reflection period' as defined by Article 13 of the CoE Convention. Trafficked victims will also be entitled to the measures contained in Article 12, paragraphs 1 and 2. Indeed, trafficked victims may be entitled to a 'residence permit' in accordance with Article 14 of the CoE Convention.

1. Each Party shall issue a renewable residence permit to victims, in one or other of the two following situations or in both:
   a. the competent authority considers that their stay is necessary owing to their personal situation;
   b. the competent authority considers that their stay is necessary for the purpose of their cooperation with the competent authorities in investigation or criminal proceedings.

A residence permit will allow a trafficked victim to stay within the destination state for a minimum period of time and is renewable. States can impose criteria for the granting of a residence permit.

According to international standards, all trafficked victims should have equal access to comprehensive assistance and protection schemes both in states of destination and states of origin upon their return. In order to meet a trafficked victim's needs and individualise the treatment, it is necessary to take into account the type of trafficking involved, the psychological characteristics of the victim and the factors in her/his social environment (Simeunovic-Patic and Copic 2010). While acknowledging that trafficking victims share some common experiences and circumstances, organisations providing assistance should recognise and respect the individuality of victims and, to the extent possible, provide personalised care and assistance (IOM 2007).

However, the capacity and capability of NRMs to effectively undertake their critical role have come under scrutiny. In the UK context, the NRM has been criticised for inconsistency and for frequent delays in making decisions as to the status of those referred to the NRM. A coalition of NGOs and lawyers published a policy document with recommendations 'to highlight the minimum standards needed for a sustainable support system towards recovery for adult survivors of slavery' (Human Trafficking Foundation 2017: 1).

The document calls for a positive decision from the NRM to carry status which is of practical assistance to the recipient in rebuilding their life, and recommends that the decision should equate to a meaningful rehabilitation period provided through the issuing of a residence permit for a minimum time period of at least 12 months. It also recommends that all potential victims be offered legal advice and representation as early in their identification as possible, and that each individual with a positive decision should be assigned a case worker who coordinates their care plan and access to services and is prepared to advocate on their behalf. (Roberts 2018: 165)

Kate Roberts from the Human Trafficking Foundation is unequivocal in her negative assessment of the UK's NRM policy.

It makes no sense that recognised victims of such a serious and debilitating crime lose their support with no guarantee of even sh-term basic needs such as secure immigration status and accommodation…This point has been described as a 'cliff edge' and does much to undermine the trust of trafficked people, as well as to expose them to destitution or further exploitation. (2018: 165)

This criticism has seemingly been accepted, belatedly, by the British government in response to a court challenge in March 2019 that the existing 45-day limit to post-NRM support causes 'irreparable harm to very vulnerable individuals' (*Independent*, 1 July 2019). In response, the Home Office accepted that the cap on support is 'incompatible with international standards' and should be based on an individual's needs rather than a stipulated length of time (*Independent* 1 July 2019). Sara Thornton, the UK's independent anti-slavery commissioner, agrees that the UK needed to improve its handling of suspected victims of modern slavery whose lives had been put 'on hold' through the lack of a timely decision on their status and hence their access to structured protection and support. With 7000 possible slavery victims identified in 2018, a figure up by a third in 2017, the identification process is struggling to cope. More than 2200 individuals who identified themselves as victims were still waiting for a decision as to their status. Thornton states that the number of victims I've met who have been waiting two or three years, for a process that is meant to take 45 days, is very troubling. And when you talk to people you get this sense of life on hold, in limbo, but also the effect on their self-esteem, their health—both mental and physical. I am concerned that the system that is set up to support and have a positive impact is actually having a negative impact in certain cases. (*Independent*, 1 March 2020)

Conclusion

The prevalence and severity of physical and psychological harm perpetrated on trafficked victims has been described as a global health concern akin in scope and impact to pandemics such as HIV/AIDS. Compounding the effects of physical and sexual violence and/or psychological persecution, victims are often coerced as part of their exploitation to commit crimes that can lead to their potential arrest and conviction. Despite provision in the CoE Convention and the Trafficking Directive for trafficked victims to be protected from prosecution for crimes committed whilst under the coercion of traffickers, there is evidence that, even amongst the authorities of EU member states, this non-punishment provision is not uniformly understood or consistently applied.

Victims are accorded specific rights in international law including privacy, confidentiality, protection of their identity and data, and access to legal services. There is evidence that the provision of these rights remains inconsistent and sporadic. Whilst there is a clear right to compensation for victims in European law, for example, there is evidence that member states rarely offer legal support for such claims. In the case of the UK, the right to claim compensation is not included in the Modern Slavery Act. Moreover, despite the protection of victims being required under international law and a panoply of related guidelines and good practice published by the UNODC and other international organisations, there is evidence that the way in which protection is delivered is inconsistent, even within a supra-national entity such as the EU. This inconsistency is apparent in the functioning of the NRMs of individual states which vary in their capacity to fulfil the critical role of identifying, protecting and assisting victims of trafficking. An underlying omission that has led to a general failure to provide adequate protection to trafficking victims is the variable awareness of governments, as well as law enforcement and criminal justice professionals of their legal obligations at transnational and national levels.

References

Council of Europe (2019), 'Anti-trafficking day: Victims must have justice, including compensation', 17 October. Available at https://www.coe.int/en/web/anti-human-trafficking/-/anti-trafficking-day-victims-must-have-justice-including-compensation-says-council-of-europe-secretary-general.

European Commission (2017), 'Communication from the Commission to the European Parliament and the Council: Reporting on the follow-up to the EU Strategy towards the Eradication of trafficking in human beings and identifying further concrete actions', December. Available at https://ec.europa.eu/anti-trafficking/sites/antitrafficking/files/20171204_communication_reporting_on_follow-up_to_the_eu_strategy_towards_the_eradication_of_trafficking_in_human_beings.pdf.

European Commission (2012), 'The EU Strategy towards the Eradication of Trafficking in Human Beings 2012–2016', June. Available at https://ec.europa.eu/anti-trafficking/sites/antitrafficking/files/eu_strategy_towards_the_eradication_of_trafficking_in_human_beings_2012-2016_1.pdf.

Fouladvand, S., and Ward, T. (2019), 'Human Trafficking, Vulnerability and the State', *Journal of Criminal Law*, Vol. 83. No. 1.

Hestia (2019), 'Underground Lives: Police responses to victims of modern slavery', March. Available at https://www.hestia.org/Handlers/Download.ashx?IDMF=952a9bfc-b57e-42f0-9ff3-6efcafb5db6f.

Independent (2020), 'Children coerced into drug trafficking face cycle of exploitation due to failings in system, warns slavery tsar'. Available at https://www.independent.co.uk/news/uk/home-news/county-lines-slavery-child-trafficking-drugs-protection-sara-thornton-a9365906.html.

Independent (2019), 'Home Office to lift cap on 'inadequate' help for trafficking victims', 1 July. Available at https://www.independent.co.uk/news/uk/home-office-modern-slavery-support-human-trafficking-smugglers-a8982746.html.

Human Trafficking Foundation (2017), 'Supporting Adult Survivors of Slavery to Facilitate Recovery and Reintegration and Prevent Re-exploitation', March. Available at http://www.humantraffickingfoundation.org/sites/default/files/Long%20term%20survivor%20support%20needs%20March%2017%202.pdf.

Inter-Agency Coordination Group against Trafficking in Persons (2012), *The International Legal Frameworks concerning Trafficking in Persons*. Vienna: ICAT

International Labour Organisation (ILO) and Walk Free Foundation (2017), *Global estimates of modern slavery: forced labour and forced marriage*. Geneva: ILO and Walk Free Foundation.

International Organisation for Migration (2007), *Direct Assistance for Victims of Trafficking*. Geneva: IOM. Available at https://publications.iom.int/system/files/pdf/iom_handbook_assistance.pdf.

Muraszkiewicz, J. M. (2019), *Protecting Victims of Human Trafficking From Liability: The European Approach*. Cham: Springer International Publishing.

Okech, D., Hansen, N., Howard, W., Anarfi, J. & Burns, A. (2018), 'Social Support, Dysfunctional Coping, and Community Reintegration as Predictors of PTSD Among Human Trafficking Survivors', *Behavioral Medicine*, Vol. 44, No. 3.

Oram, S. et al. (2016), 'Human Trafficking and Health: A Survey of Male and Female Survivors in England', *American Journal of Public Health*, Vol. 106, No. 6.

Organization for Security and Cooperation in Europe (2013a), 'Policy and legislative recommendations towards the effective implementation of the non-punishment provision with regard to victims of trafficking', April. Available at http://lastradainternational.org/lsidocs/Effective%20recommendation%20of%20the%20non-punishment%20provision.pdf.

Organization for Security and Cooperation in Europe (2014), *National Referral Mechanisms: Joining Efforts to Protect the Rights of Trafficked Persons A Practical Handbook*. Warsaw: OSCE Office for Democratic Institutions and Human Rights.

Pearson, E. (2002), *Human traffic, human rights: redefining victim protection*. London: Anti-Slavery International. Available at http://www.antislavery.org/wp-content/uploads/2017/01/hum_traff_hum_rights_redef_vic_protec_final_full.pdf.

Roberts, K. (2018), 'Life after Trafficking: A gap in UK's modern slavery efforts', *Anti-Trafficking Review*, No. 10. Available at http://www.antitraffickingreview.org/index.php/atrjournal/article/view/329.

Simeunovic-Patic, B., and Copic, S. (2010), 'Protection and Assistance to Victims of Human Trafficking in Serbia: Recent Developments', European Journal of Criminology, Vol. 7, No. 1.

United Nations Office on Drugs and Crime (2014), *SOP Manual for Law Enforcement Personnel of the Central Asia countries on the cases related to human trafficking and smuggling of migrants*. Vienna: UNODC.

Villacampo, C. and Torres, N. (2019), 'Human trafficking for criminal exploitation: Effects suffered by victims in their passage through the criminal justice system', *International Review of Victimology*, Vol. 25, No. 1.

Zimmerman C., and Kiss, L. (2017), 'Human trafficking and exploitation: A global health concern', *PLoS Medical*, Vol. 14, No. 11.

5

Preventing Human Trafficking

Abstract The chapter analyses strategies, both general and specific, aimed at the pre-emptive prevention of human trafficking, focussing particularly on education and consciousness-raising campaigns. It finds that there is evidence that individual projects and prevention strategies often suffer from either no evaluation, or unscientific evaluation. Unproductive evaluation prevents the development of evidence-based approaches to countering human trafficking, and inhibits lesson learning. Moreover, the divergent interpretations of human trafficking in different jurisdictions, analysed in preceding chapters, can lead to preventive training reinforcing a disparate, rather than unified, international response to countering human trafficking.

Keywords: Prevention campaigns • Evaluation • Data collection

An effective prevention strategy should be comprehensive and coordinate stakeholders tasked with countering the threat. Other elements of counter-trafficking, notably protection and prosecution, are intrinsically linked with prevention. Effective protection of vulnerable individuals can

© The Author(s) 2020
S. Massey, G. Rankin, *Exploiting People for Profit*,
https://doi.org/10.1057/978-1-137-43413-5_5

prevent them from being coerced into a trafficking situation, whilst the protection of those who have already been the victims of trafficking can prevent re-victimisation. Likewise, successful and high-profile prosecutions can both deter traffickers and raise awareness of the threat amongst potential trafficking victims.

There are, however, specific strategies that fall under the discrete category of 'prevention'. These strategies, for the most part, fall on the supply side and seek to inhibit the factors that lead to individuals falling prey to trafficking and are directed primarily at vulnerable populations and avenues of recruitment and transport. Prevention strategies can be categorised into two main areas. Firstly, the targeted pursuit of traffickers intended to deter trafficking activity. Secondly, the establishment of the capacity to identify and prevent possible trafficking scenarios before they occur. Some countries and jurisdictions, for example, the Nordic countries in the context of trafficking for sexual exploitation, have also sought to formulate strategies that target the demand for the services provided by trafficking victims.

The chapter assesses the scope of anti-trafficking knowledge dissemination, comparing the relative effectiveness of prevention and awareness-raising strategies. Using case studies including the authors' own experiences of practical prevention strategies such as the EU-funded Migration Aware campaign in Nigeria, the chapter examines the relevance of prevention and awareness-raising campaigns, their purpose, impact and effectiveness. The chapter further assesses the ethical and political drivers behind the push-and-pull factors and how these factors influence the development of effective prevention strategies in the context of the often divergent, and sometimes conflicting, agendas of the states of origin and destination.

What Is Prevention?

The complexity of human trafficking requires that efforts to prevent human trafficking from taking place should be evidence-based and driven by a response to credible data rather than assumptions. Many national strategies are undertaken without adequate research and are not effectively monitored or evaluated to assess their effectiveness and impact. Article 5 of the CoE Convention requires individual States Parties to develop a portfolio of relevant inter-agency initiatives to prevent human trafficking taking place (see Box 5.1).

Box 5.1 Prevention of trafficking in human beings

Chapter II
Prevention, cooperation and other measures

Article 5
Prevention of trafficking in human beings

1. Each Party shall take measures to establish or strengthen national coordination between the various bodies responsible for preventing and combating trafficking in human beings.
2. Each Party shall establish and/or strengthen effective policies and programmes to prevent trafficking in human beings, by such means as: research, information, awareness raising and education campaigns, social and economic initiatives and training programmes, in particular for persons vulnerable to trafficking and for professionals concerned with trafficking in human beings.
3. Each Party shall promote a Human Rights-based approach and shall use gender mainstreaming and a child-sensitive approach in the development, implementation and assessment of all the policies and programmes referred to in paragraph 2.
4. Each Party shall take appropriate measures, as may be necessary, to enable migration to take place legally, in particular through dissemination of accurate information by relevant offices, on the conditions enabling the legal entry in and stay on its territory.
5. Each Party shall take specific measures to reduce children's vulnerability to trafficking, notably by creating a protective environment for them.
6. Measures established in accordance with this article shall involve, where appropriate, non-governmental organisations, other relevant organisations and other elements of civil society committed to the prevention of trafficking in human beings and victim protection or assistance.

(continued)

Box 5.1 (continued)

Article 6
Measures to discourage the demand

To discourage the demand that fosters all forms of exploitation of persons, especially women and children, that leads to trafficking, each Party shall adopt or strengthen legislative, administrative, educational, social, cultural or other measures including:

a. research on best practices, methods and strategies;
b. raising awareness of the responsibility and important role of media and civil society in identifying the demand as one of the root causes of trafficking in human beings;
c. target information campaigns involving, as appropriate, inter alia, public authorities and policy makers;
d. preventive measures, including educational programmes for boys and girls during their schooling, which stress the unacceptable nature of discrimination based on sex, and its disastrous consequences, the importance of gender equality and the dignity and integrity of every human being.

Source: Council of Europe Convention on Action against Trafficking in Human Beings (2005)

The Trafficking Directive also includes specific provisions on the prevention of human trafficking. Similar to the CoE Convention, the Directive requires member states to take organise consciousness-raising, awareness, education and training initiatives and campaigns. Where appropriate, these campaigns should be organised in cooperation with relevant civil society organisations and other stakeholders. Such preventative action should be aimed at ensuring a broad understanding within society of the threat posed by human trafficking in order to reduce the risk of people, including children, becoming victims of human trafficking for want of accurate information. Yet, the EU Strategy published in 2012 recognises that

> numerous anti-trafficking prevention programmes, in particular awareness-raising campaigns, have been implemented locally, nationally, internationally and in third countries. However, little has been done to systematically evaluate the impact of such prevention programmes in terms of their

achieving their objectives, such as changes in behaviour and attitudes, thus reducing the likelihood of trafficking in human beings. Little is also known about the added value, coherence and consistency (where appropriate) of such initiatives and the links between them. (2012: 8)

Whilst critiquing their effectiveness, the EU Strategy acknowledges that pursuit and prosecution is an insufficient response to human trafficking and that prevention strategies should be developed to reflect and address the 'root causes' of trafficking in EU and third countries (2012: 7).

However, the EU has ostensibly downgraded prevention as a policy priority since the 2012–2016 Strategy concluded. A communication from the EU Commission to the European Parliament and EU Council in December 2017 declared the five key priorities of the EU Strategy—prevention, prosecution, protection of victims, partnerships and improving knowledge—as having been implemented (EU Commission 2017). Implicitly accepting the limited effectiveness of the Strategy, the communication cites the global financial crisis, the migration crisis and security threats posed by organised crime groups as having set further challenges to addressing the threat posed by human trafficking. Making human trafficking a priority crime threat area in the 2018–2021 EU Policy Cycle on Organised and Serious International Crime, the Commission proposes three key areas to strengthen preventive measures through cross-cutting action.

The first, 'disrupting the business model and untangling the trafficking chain', further prompts EU member states, to the extent they have not done so, to criminalise those knowingly using services exacted from victims of trafficking (EU Commission 2017: 3–4). Further, the Commission seeks to encourage and assist EU national authorities in their concrete initiatives to disrupt the financial business model and to encourage and assist member states to make investigations and prosecutions more effective through capacity building, development of tools, information exchange and sharing best practice, and law enforcement and judicial cooperation, including promoting the setting up of Joint Investigation Teams (JITs) both within the EU and with non-EU countries (EU Commission 2017: 3–4). In terms of the private and non-governmental sectors, the Commission seeks the promotion of sustainable business practices and working conditions in production countries; and to promote best practice and training sessions with relevant national authorities, businesses and civil society, especially on applying the guidelines on the methodology for reporting non-financial information that includes trafficking in human beings (EU Commission 2017: 3–4).

The second key area, to 'provide better access to and realise the rights for victims', will publish guidance to member states on gender-specific measures for helping and supporting victims and develop practical guidance to enhance inter-agency and transnational cooperation aiming to prevent child trafficking of EU children (EU Commission 2017: 4–6). Recognising that the onus for the delivery of protection to victims lies with individual member states, the Commission proposes a review of the functioning of the national referral mechanisms and a focus on capacity building to improve cooperation by means of EU border and migration management tools for detecting, identifying and sharing information and data on victims of trafficking and traffickers (EU Commission 2017: 4–6). In terms of constructing a holistic approach with EU member states to address human trafficking, the Commission will continue to advise national authorities on key concepts relating to trafficking in human beings, to help improve operational work, policy development, data comparability and reporting (EU Commission 2017: 4–6).

The third priority, to 'intensify a coordinated and consolidated response, both within and outside the EU', requires the EU agencies to ameliorate the push factors that lead to individuals becoming vulnerable to trafficking including reviewing and identifying priority countries and regions for action against trafficking in human beings, working towards achieving Agenda 2030 Sustainable Development Goals, and promoting a renewed commitment by EU Justice and Home Affairs agencies to working together against trafficking (EU Commission 2017: 6–7). In terms of prioritising the gendered dimension of human trafficking, the Commission will seek to ensure that the components of the European Union—United Nations Spotlight Initiative—to eliminate violence against women and girls are implemented, that the measures relating to trafficking in human beings included in the document 'The EU's Activities on Gender Equality and Women's Empowerment in the EU's External Relations' are implemented, and that the commitments made under the

Call to Action on Protection from Gender-Based Violence in Emergencies are met (EU Commission 2017: 6–7).

If no longer a discrete priority, the EU Commission's approach to prevention continues its outsourcing policy, and the Commission's communication identifies a number of entities and initiatives it supports that meet its 'anti-trafficking objectives and priorities, including projects taking particular account of the gender dimension of the phenomenon [and] high-risk groups as well as high-risk sectors' (European Commission 2017: 8). These projects include the Asylum Migration & Integration Fund (AMIF), the Internal Security Fund (ISF) Police & Borders, Horizon 2020, the EU Framework Programme for Research and Innovation, Justice Programme and Rights, Equality & Citizenship Programme, European Neighbourhood Instrument (ENI), Instrument for Pre-accession Assistance (IPA), Mobility Partnership Facility, the European Development Fund, the Development Cooperation Instrument, the EU Instrument contributing to Stability & Peace (IcSP), and the EU Emergency Trust Fund for Africa (European Commission 2017: 8).

There is evidence that these campaigns fail to prevent trafficking as they tackle the symptoms rather than the underlying 'root causes'—the push-and-pull factors and the fundamental driver of national and, in the case of the EU, supra-national immigration policies (Nieuwenhuys and Pécoud 2007). In many instances, these campaigns, usually paid for by the destination states or the EU, are taken to be a form of 'delocalized migration control' intended to dissuade any attempt at migration rather than explicitly to prevent trafficking.

> Although not coercive, the discouragement of potential migrants indeed raises the issue of the boundary between dissuasion and interdiction. Information campaigns may prefigure an era of control in which a kind of interdiction to leave, through subtle and hidden pressures on sending countries and social actors involved in migration, will be indirectly reintroduced. (Nieuwenhuys and Pécoud 2007: 1691)

Emphasising the complexity of human trafficking as a crime and as a social phenomenon, the UK's ATMG maintains that in order for prevention to work, a holistic approach that acknowledges and encompasses economic, social, psychological, cultural and political factors is required

(2012: 4). A comprehensive prevention strategy should be conceptualised simultaneously at three levels—primary, secondary and tertiary—in order to effectively target issues surrounding supply and demand at all stages of trafficking in the states of both origin and destination. Primary level prevention interventions are fundamental and aimed at a wide audience, secondary level prevention is aimed at specific high-risk groups, whilst tertiary level prevention takes place once trafficking has already taken place with a view to avoid further harm.

Similarly, activities undertaken as part of prevention strategies can vary from short-term training exercises, through medium-term activities such as courses and programmes, to long-term approaches such as government policy interventions. However, in order to effectively address the deep roots of human trafficking, the ATMG cautions that

> all three levels of prevention must be addressed. In order to achieve this, specific prevention measures need to be implemented at various points in both source and destination countries: amongst the general population, within targeted sectors of society and labour markets, and at domestic and international policy level. (2012: 5)

Prevention strategies should focus their key messages at specific target groups. These may be broad, such as the general public, or more targeted, such as young people leaving education, jobless and/or homeless individuals, or ethnic minorities. Moreover, in terms of transnational trafficking, key messages and the most effective channels for dissemination of these messages should be identified in conjunction with anti-trafficking organisations in the state of origin.

At the primary level, the approach taken includes widespread education campaigns about human trafficking which might be incorporated in the national education curriculum of the states of both origin and destination or be aimed at the wider public. Appropriate channels to reach the target groups might include the printed media, educator-led discussions in schools around information leaflets and case studies, television and radio programmes, as well as public service advertising.

The secondary level targets high-risk groups, and might include bespoke initiatives such as 'programmes to encourage vulnerable young people to remain in education, and information campaigns for migrants on safe migration, or their rights in destination countries and skills training for employment' (ATMG 2012: 4). In order to have impact, campaigns at this level should be based on a comprehensive understanding of the sending society. Channels to reach high-risk groups might include radio broadcasts in local languages, leaflets in migrant languages in supermarkets, particularly cheap supermarkets, leaflets in appropriate languages in seat pockets of budget airlines, advertisements in free or cheap newspapers, campaigns and meetings organised by diplomatic missions of destination states in states of origin, and poster campaigns including at points of entry to the destination state such as toilets at airports or bus stations. Core information disseminated might include the coercive techniques used by traffickers, labour and migration rights in the country of destination, and contact information for anti-trafficking support agencies in the states of both origin and destination.

The focus of the tertiary stage of a prevention strategy is dealing with trafficking once it has already occurred. There is a strong overlap at this point with protection, in particular preventing re-trafficking. Key to achieving this goal is effective identification of trafficking victims and effective referral to NRMs for appropriate protection and care.

Prevention Strategies

Any prevention strategy is only one strand of a comprehensive response to human trafficking and must also link with other counter-trafficking elements, notably investigation, prosecution and protection. Such strategies, for the most part, fall on the supply side and seek to inhibit the factors that lead to individuals becoming prey to trafficking, as well as targeting vulnerable populations and avenues of recruitment and transport. Prevention strategies can be categorised into four areas. Firstly, a policy-driven ambition to radically change the overall context in which human trafficking takes place and/or the environment in which it occurs. Secondly, a more focused response to the discrete variables that contribute to the risk and/or vulnerability of individuals or groups that can lead to trafficking. Thirdly, the targeted pursuit of traffickers intended to deter trafficking activity. Finally, to establish the capacity to identify and prevent possible trafficking scenarios before they occur.

As with the other elements of an effective counter-trafficking strategy, prevention should be concentrated on the victim in the context of a human rights approach. Those involved with developing prevention methodologies should seek to involve the target groups in the design and evaluation of prevention initiatives, focus on the location of exploitation, link protection and prevention actions, tackle the causes of exploitation and, if appropriate, ensure that the strategy is child and gender sensitive. The strategy should also set itself clear objectives for its component initiatives. For example, is the priority to raise awareness in the countries of origin or destination, or is it to reduce supply or demand? Prevention campaigns fail, or are less impactful, when their focus has been on the symptoms of human trafficking rather than on underlying structural factors (see Box 5.2). The targets of prevention campaigns struggle to engage with campaigns that ignore the fundamental drivers behind their own circumstances.

Box 5.2 'Migration Aware'—irregular migration: Filling the information gap

Case Study: Migration Aware

Migration Aware was a limited project that formed part of the multi-strand Migration for Development (M4D) initiative funded by the EU and administered by the UN Development Programme (UNDP). Based in Ibadan, Nigeria, the purpose of the project was to deliver an awareness campaign aimed at potential irregular migrants in order to enable them to make an informed decision about migrating across land and sea borders without valid documentation migration.

Following a scoping study, focus groups, and stakeholder meetings, the project set itself the target, agreed with project managers from the UNDP, to ensure that 10 percent of the population of Ibadan aged 16–25, the demographic most likely to consider irregular migration, was exposed to at least one of the project's dissemination methodologies. This amounted to reaching 26,000 people aged 16–25.

Ultimately, five key methodologies were chosen to disseminate information on the potential risks of irregular migration by land and sea, including the risk of becoming a victim of human trafficking.

• A poster campaign
• Street theatre performances
• SMS text-messaging campaign
• Drama-documentary

(continued)

Box 5.2 (continued)

Against the criterion of numerical reach, the campaign achieved its over-arching target. Three of the methodologies proved successful, at least in terms of number of individuals from the target demographic being exposed to the methodologies' messages. Despite the prevalence of mobile phones amongst the youth demographic, technical limitations at the time meant that the commercial telecoms company hired to send the bulk messages could only offer an arbitrary service that failed to focus the bulk messages on the youth demographic in Ibadan. The poster campaign emphasised the need for cultural sensitivity with the UK and Nigerian partners working together to find a balance between visual and verbal graphic design. Likewise, the street theatre performances prioritised local expertise in terms of how to disseminate information effectively to the target demographic and the nature of the information being conveyed. The drama documentary was the most expensive, but also by far the most successful single methodology in terms of reach. Drawing on the street theatre performances, a half hour drama-documentary was produced again drawing on local technical and creative expertise. That the numerical target for the project was reached was largely down to the broadcast of the drama-documentary on regional television, the Broadcasting Corporation of Oyo State (BCOS).

Superficially successful, the Migration Aware project, nonetheless, replicated the common error of focussing on symptoms rather than causes. Reasons for this include the lack of coordination with similar projects in Nigeria and elsewhere, both within the context of the wider Migration for development initiative and/or funded by other donors, as well as the relative lack of resources to attempt to fundamentally influence underlying causes rather than warn potential migrants. However, the main lesson learned from the project was the importance of constructing a comprehensive and responsive monitoring and evaluation regime for the project so that mistakes could be rectified quickly and that, in the medium-term, project successes could be replicated and errors avoided.

Source: Migration for Development. Available at: http://www.migration 4development.org/en/projects/migration-aware-irregular-migration-filling-information-gap

The UN and EU are often the initiators of preventive action, although specific measures and initiatives are usually outsourced to NGOs and/or the private sector, as was the case with the Migration Aware campaign (see Box 5.2). There is a clear need for coherence and joined-up management of prevention activities. Prevention campaigns are often under-resourced and consciousness-raising initiatives often fail to reach either the target group or the general public in the states of origin and/or destination, to train practitioners and administrators, or to undertake the depth of research required to develop evidence-based responses. Recognising that specific research into the effectiveness of prevention strategies remains scarce, Kiss and Zimmerman revisit their recommendation that human trafficking should be treated as a global health concern. In this context, they propose that 'prevention and intervention approaches should, therefore, draw on and learn from approaches and methods used in the evaluation of other population health risks such as violence, smoking, and obesity' (2019: 1–2). Despite the current limitations of research into prevention strategies, Kiss and Zimmerman point to emerging evidence that accepted prevention measures may be unhelpful and even harmful.For instance, emerging findings from the field suggest that there may be limited benefit in 'awareness-raising' interventions and indicate possible unintended harm from training courses that are not solidly grounded in contextual evidence. These findings confirm the need for a systematic integrated approach across the migration pathway that addresses structural conditions in addition to individual-level behaviours and risks. (Kiss and Zimmerman 2019: 2)

The lack of scientific evaluation of the value of prevention and awareness-raising campaigns in the area of human trafficking fosters further chronic underfunding as donors are unwilling to fund campaigns whose outcomes cannot be predicted or performance improved. In the European context, the Commission has re-emphasised the need for member states to draw on expertise already available within Eurojust and Europol.

One of the most persistent issues on the human trafficking agenda has been the lack of robust data collection and focused research. A deficiency of specialised knowledge and expertise hinders the effective implementation of anti-trafficking policies and strategies. Without a strong evidence base, policies often follow political, economic and/or social agendas. Yet gathering accurate data is time-consuming and expensive and requires a sustained effort as the *modus operandi* of the traffickers constantly responds to the strategies and tactics employed by law enforcement and criminal justice authorities. In the context of the definition of human trafficking, it is essential to understand what makes people vulnerable to violence, abuse and exploitation in the first place in order to successfully assist vulnerable individuals and communities to protect themselves from potentially harmful situations. Thus, preventing human trafficking is largely predicated on reducing vulnerability and providing alternatives to the inducements of the traffickers. Understanding vulnerability and the abuse of power connected to vulnerability is vital for the development of successful strategies against human trafficking.

Moreover, whilst seeking a cohesive response to a complex and changing criminal phenomenon, the EU must manage divergent capabilities, capacities and policy priorities amongst their diverse membership. As an organisation, the EU is reliant on training and capacity-building exercises, incorporating state and non-state stakeholders, to build coherence and good practice in the investigation and prosecution of cases of human trafficking, and an appropriate response to the victims of trafficking.

A further obstacle to preventing human trafficking is the widespread unfamiliarity with the specifics of the crime outside of specialist law enforcement and criminal justice agencies. As a result, criminal activity that falls within the definition of human trafficking and for which there are remedies under human trafficking law are often not recognised as such and are dealt with as other crimes, or not addressed at all. Moreover, the general public and, often, the key public sector bodies are largely unaware of the underlying causes, severity and widespread nature of the problem. This has resulted in only limited action being taken against the organised criminals.

In the UK context, a study by the ATMG assesses the record of recent Conservative governments' policy emphasis on addressing human trafficking and modern slavery. It concludes that whilst the governance framework has expanded and there are more organisations focused on addressing human trafficking, there is an 'absence of a comprehensive UK prevention strategy and lack of strategic focus' leading to these efforts being 'disjointed and siloed' (ATMG 2018: 78). In particular,to ensure that efforts to prevent trafficking honour the human rights of trafficked persons, the Government should urgently review other areas of policy and legislation that affect trafficked persons. Prevention must become an integral part of anti-trafficking policy in the UK, with a primary focus on reducing the vulnerabilities of trafficked children and adults, as well as those at risk of trafficking. (ATMG 2018: 79)

There is a growing recognition that for prevention strategies to work, there is a need to ensure exchange of good practice and cooperation and coordination between states and across regions. It has been recognised as crucial to ensure a sustained and long-term response to human trafficking and to guarantee that the funding of initiatives results in appropriate interventions based on well-tested project plans. In addition, international cooperation helps to ensure that isolated responses to the crime do not simply result in the problem being diverted elsewhere. Combating human trafficking requires a capacity to implement a comprehensive preventive approach both domestically and transnationally. In most cases, individual states want to take action against human trafficking, but are deterred by lack of resources, capacity and/or expertise. Effective coordination should result in demonstrable mutual benefit.

Monitoring and Evaluating Prevention Strategies

Explaining, understanding and capturing 'impact' have become a prerequisite of organisations and individuals from government to civil society. However, efforts to tackle human trafficking in Europe are relatively recent and have not, as yet, been subjected to rigorous impact evaluation. Developing an effective monitoring and evaluation regime is hampered by the lack of coherence and/or consistency in the objectives of prevention initiatives, particularly concerning which groups will be affected, through what means and in what ways. Consequently, there is only limited systematic research into the impacts of anti-trafficking initiatives. Such research has been avoided due to its inherent expense and difficulty, and has been hindered by problems of methodological nationalism, the absence of a comparative dimension and difficulties in tracing impact. There also exist ambiguities in comparing divergent types of preventative campaigns such as projects which aim to improve prevention strategies, campaigns that aim to raise awareness, training exercises and combinations of each of these approaches. This complexity is exacerbated by the tendency for campaigns to incorporate a range of governmental and non-governmental actors and organisations which often have competing and overlapping objectives. Writing in 2005, Frank Laczko, currently the director of the IOM's Global Data Analysis Centre (GMDAC), argued that there had been only limited independent evaluation of policies and programmes intended to prevent human trafficking on which to assess the real impact and effectiveness of the range of interventions. He noted at the time that much of the research on which preventive measures are predicated is action-oriented and intended to prepare the ground for counter-trafficking interventions. Given the increasing domestic and international pressure to effectively address human trafficking, this research is often time-constrained, but also under-resourced. Focusing on the reliability and utility of data in 2005, Laczko noted that there was only limited research to thoroughly determine the effectiveness of prevention strategies over time, or longitudinal research assessing the before, during and after of interventions. Moreover, the impact of prevention projects up to 2005 had proved difficult to measure. Arguably, a majority of these initiatives failed to achieve their stated aims as they concentrated predominantly on the symptoms rather than the root causes of human trafficking. Laczko argued that it was important to 'move beyond stating that trafficking is a problem to assessing in more detail how well we are dealing with this problem' (2005: 14).

> Policy approaches should become more evidence-based, drawing on the results of relevant research and evaluations…There is a need for donors to give much greater priority to evaluation research, which can help to determine the effectiveness of different programmes and policy approaches. (Laczko 2005: 14)

Thirteen years after this analysis, Laczko, together with colleagues from GMDAC, revisited the record of prevention initiatives. This new study comprises a meta-analysis of the evaluation of 60 prevention campaigns, mainly 'workshop-type activities and cable TV programmes/advertisements' with the most seeking to mitigate human trafficking. Despite the majority of these evaluations self-assessing their campaigns as 'successful', the IOM team was sceptical. According to the IOM's analysis, 'impact', in the sense of 'a change in outcome that is directly attributable to the programme and not any other factor', is not directly measured by these evaluations (Tjaden et al. 2018: 7). More fundamentally, 'most of the evaluations identified did not meet minimum standards for robust evidence on programme effects' (Tjaden et al. 2018: 7).The GMDAC's findings have been substantiated by a further meta-analysis undertaken by Deanna Davy who found thatdespite rapid growth in the number of programmes at the international, regional, national, and local levels that aim to prevent and combat human trafficking, protect victims, and prosecute traffickers, there has been a limited attempt to comprehensively evaluate anti–human trafficking programs and their effectiveness. (2016: 501)

Davy points to numerous shortcomings in the 49 evaluations reviewed for her study. These include confusion between monitoring and evaluation, a dearth of rigorous evaluations, failure to assess whether, and to what extent, programme aims and objectives are reached, a short-term focus, failure to evaluate cost efficiency, failure to include victims in data collection processes, and the limited number of evaluations of legislation and prosecutions to combat human trafficking. She is critical of the way in which many of the evaluations were conducted 'in-house' arguing that 'transparency is crucial to the credibility of evaluations, which means not only having impartial evaluators conduct the evaluations but also making the evaluation frameworks, findings, and recommendations made public' (2016: 501). The utility of evaluations of anti-human trafficking campaigns published in peer-reviewed journals has also been questioned by Natalia Szablewska and Krzysztof Kubacki who argue that none of the 16 studies that met their predetermined search criteria are actually evaluative as they fail to include outcome, process or impact evaluations (2018: 118). From an action-oriented perspective, there is a need across multiple sectors for independent evaluations of 'what works and what does not, rather than expanding the number of opinion-based studies, which are of limited guidance to practice in this area' (Szablewska and Kubacki 2018: 119).

Conclusion

Preventing human trafficking from taking place by disseminating knowledge and information to forewarn potential victims and by enhancing the capacity of domestic and international law enforcement and criminal justice agencies to address the threat is a sensible, cost-effective and fundamental part of a holistic counter-trafficking strategy. The notion of prevention, however, covers multiple aspirations on the part of international and national donors. These include consciousness-raising campaigns for the general public to more focused awareness exercises aimed at the spectrum of vulnerable individuals and demographic groupings, education and training across the public and private sectors, the collection of accurate data to inform evidence-based policy formulation, as well as macro foreign policy and development strategies to mitigate push factors in the countries of origin.

Yet, at present, common and accepted strategies for preventing trafficking are often not rigorously evaluated, lessons not learnt and good practice not disseminated. There is growing evidence that awareness-raising campaigns might have limited value in preventing the incidence of trafficking. Moreover, in the absence of a shared understanding of the criminality involved in human trafficking or a universally recognised strategy to counter the threat, the training of law enforcement and criminal justice operatives is often disparate and, rather than promoting unanimity, potentially encourages divergence in the approaches taken to address the crime by individual jurisdictions.

References

Anti-Trafficking Monitoring Group (2012), 'All Change: Preventing Trafficking in the UK', April. Available at https://www.amnesty.org.uk/files/all_change_report.pdf.

Anti-Trafficking Monitoring Group (2018), 'Before the Harm is Done: Examining the UK's response to the prevention of trafficking', September. Available at https://www.antislavery.org/wp-content/uploads/2018/09/Before-the-Harm-is-Done-report.pdf.

Davy, D. (2016), 'Anti–Human Trafficking Interventions: How Do We Know if They Are Working?' *American Journal of Evaluation*, Vol. 37, No. 4.

European Commission (2017), 'Communication from the Commission to the European Parliament and the Council: Reporting on the follow-up to the EU Strategy towards the Eradication of trafficking in human beings and identifying further concrete actions', December. Available at https://ec.europa.eu/anti-trafficking/sites/antitrafficking/files/20171204_communication_reporting_on_follow-up_to_the_eu_strategy_towards_the_eradication_of_trafficking_in_human_beings.pdf.

European Commission (2012), 'The EU Strategy towards the Eradication of Trafficking in Human Beings 2012–2016', June. Available at https://ec.europa.eu/anti-trafficking/sites/antitrafficking/files/eu_strategy_towards_the_eradication_of_trafficking_in_human_beings_2012-2016_1.pdf.

Kiss, L., and Zimmerman, C., (2019), 'Human trafficking and labor exploitation: Toward identifying, implementing, and evaluating effective responses', *PLoS Medical*, Vol. 16, No. 1.

Laczko, F. (2005), 'Introduction', in Laczko, F., and Gozdziak, E. *Data and Research on Human Trafficking: A Global Survey Offprint of the Special Issue of International Migration*. Geneva: IOM.

Nieuwenhuys, C., and Pécoud, A. (2007), 'Human trafficking, information campaigns, and strategies of migration control', *American Behavioral Scientist*, No. 50.

Szablewska, N., Kubacki, K. (2018), 'Anti-Human Trafficking Campaigns: A Systematic Literature Review', *Social Marketing Quarterly*, Vol. 24, No. 2.

Tjaden, J., Morgenstern, S., Laczko, F. (2018), 'Evaluating the impact of information campaigns in the field of migration: A systematic review of the evidence, and practical guidance', *Central Mediterranean Route Thematic Report Series*, No. 1. Available at http://www.eapmigrationpanel.org/sites/default/files/evaluating_the_impact_of_information_campaigns_in_field_of_migration_iom_gmdac.pdf.

Concluding Remarks

Whilst the exploitation of people for labour and sex has been a constant throughout history, human trafficking as an offence in international law was only defined as recently as 2000. The adoption of the Trafficking Protocol stimulated a growing awareness by the government, law enforcement and criminal justice agencies, the non-governmental sector and the general public of the threat posed by human trafficking. However, the difficulties inherent in collecting accurate data have, most likely, led to the scale and scope of human trafficking being underestimated. The British government, for example, whilst still unable to provide definitive figures, has substantially raised its estimate from 13,000 to tens of thousands of trafficked victims in the UK. This rise can be partially explained by a better understanding of labour exploitation and the number of people trafficked for their labour. Until recent times, policy and prevention focus was disproportionately on trafficking for sexual exploitation.

Calculating the numbers being trafficked is also complicated by definitional confusion. In particular, the crimes of human trafficking and the smuggling of migrants are often conflated not only by the media and the public, but also by the authorities in individual jurisdictions. Whilst the distinction between trafficking and smuggling is distinct in the Protocols, there is growing evidence that on the migrant journey, the business of

© The Author(s) 2020
S. Massey, G. Rankin, *Exploiting People for Profit*,
https://doi.org/10.1057/978-1-137-43413-5

smuggling people across borders can readily transmute into the crime of exploiting people for profit. Moreover, there is a case made in the scholarly literature for push factors such as extreme poverty and the absence of life opportunities to be acknowledged in international law as equally coercive as the threats and deceptions practised by traffickers. Yet, developed world states have no incentive to reappraise the legal *status quo* since, at present, those found to be trafficked must in law be protected and supported, whilst those found to be smuggled are categorised as criminals liable to detention and deportation.

What is becoming clearer, however, is the amount of illicit earnings being generated by the crime of human trafficking in all its forms. Considered the third most lucrative organised criminal activity after drug and arms trafficking, it is estimated to turn over $150 billion for the criminals involved. The aim of this short book has been to gauge the current status of efforts at the national, regional and international levels to counter human trafficking.

Fundamental to an effective response is a clear and cohesive pattern of legal remedies that cascade from international legal treaties, conventions and protocols to the legal systems of states of origin, transit and destination. Despite the criticism it has attracted, the Trafficking Protocol was a crucial juncture in the fight against human trafficking when it was adopted in 2000. Since then, 174 UN member states have ratified the Protocol, agreeing to establish an offence of human trafficking in their domestic legal systems. Critics have stressed the Protocol's omissions, the absence of clear specific explanations of key terms related to the definition of human trafficking, recruitment, deception, coercion and exploitation. In particular, the absence of clear definitions of the three elements that comprise the process of human trafficking—action, means and purpose—leads to discrete interpretations of these concepts in the legislation of individual jurisdictions which hinder the adoption of a universal understanding of what constitutes the offence of human trafficking. These ambiguities arguably weaken its utility as a practical mechanism to counter human trafficking. In the absence of a treaty body, the UNODC, as the intergovernmental agency tasked with coordinating the international response to human trafficking as a crime and concept, has struggled to enforce a cohesive understanding in the face of the diverse agendas of states and regions.

Ambiguous interpretations of the definition of human trafficking in international law can lead to inaccurate identification of trafficked victims. Moreover, deconstructing the complex motivations of often traumatised and suspicious migrants requires specialist expertise that is often in limited supply. Similar limitations restrict the number of pro-active, intelligence-led counter-trafficking operations using specialist SIT techniques that law enforcement agencies have the resources to conduct. This is applicable in developed world countries, but even more relevant in jurisdictions in the developing world. Management of human trafficking cases by investigators and prosecutors should be concentrated on the sympathetic, yet effective, management of victims as complainants and witnesses. Whilst some practitioners advocate wider use of SIT to avoid the intrinsic difficulties and uncertainties of handling victims, the increased use of SIT brings problems of cost, advanced technical capabilities and potential legal constraints on the use of invasive surveillance. It also further marginalises individuals from a process which, whilst nominally 'victim-centred', is often more concerned with securing a conviction than upholding victim rights.

The scope and scale of physical and psychological abuse sustained by human trafficking victims across the globe is of such a magnitude that it has been equated to global pandemics. This suffering is often made worse by the criminalisation of victims for offences committed under coercion whilst being trafficked. The protection of victim rights in international law is addressed in the Trafficking Protocol, and in the European context, in the CoE Convention and the Trafficking Directive. Yet, in practice, the rights of trafficked victims are often not respected, and, more fundamentally, not always understood by those tasked with investigating and prosecuting trafficking cases.

A key tool employed by OSCE member states, and other states, to ensure the rights of trafficked victims and provide tangible protection and support is the national referral mechanism. Yet, the record of NRMs in meeting their specific objectives is inconsistent. In theory, a state's principal instrument for the protection of rights, NRMs could potentially deliver a full spectrum of support services to victims. However, the effectiveness of an individual NRM relies on political will and must be compatible with the priorities of current counter-trafficking and immigration policies, the specifics of an individual state's implementation strategy and the availability of human and physical capital. Often underfunded and/or under-publicised to victims, NRMs frequently fail to reach a significant proportion of victims. Decisions concerning an individual's designation as a trafficking victim can take a long time. Moreover, the services which NRMs are tasked to provide may be restricted to, for example, victims of sex trafficking, but not victims of trafficking for labour exploitation. Services offered to those designated as victims can also be time-limited, providing protection for a short period, but then leaving the victim without adequate support, notably access to secure accommodation.

Human trafficking is a highly complex crime. This applies both in terms of the specific criminality involved and in how that criminality is framed in international law and national law. The pursuit of those who commit the crime of human trafficking is an obligation for all states that claim to uphold the rule of law and as a deterrent to would-be traffickers. However, SITs including advanced surveillance, financial investigation and forensic accountancy are both expensive and hence, usually, limited to developed world states able to afford to train and deploy expert personnel. Given that human trafficking frequently has a transnational dimension, it is often more effective, in developing and developed world states, to use more traditional, less invasive law enforcement and criminal justice methods and approaches.

A fundamental requirement for an effective counter-trafficking strategy is unanimity of purpose. This should include a common interpretation of international law as it applies to human trafficking, notably the Trafficking Protocol, translated, if necessary, into corresponding national legislation. This should be reinforced with equivalent government strategies, interoperable implementation means and methods, intelligence sharing and knowledge exchange, investigative, prosecutorial and juridical mutual assistance, and common regulatory regimes. In essence, *partnership*—global, regional and within nation-states—is the underpinning methodology most likely to effectively counter the criminality and consequences of human trafficking.

The region most advanced in effectuating practicable collaborative institutions and mechanisms across these sectors in order to facilitate investigation and prosecution is the EU. Nonetheless, as tacitly acknowledged in the review of the EU 2012–2016 Strategy, human trafficking remains a potent and, probably, growing threat in Europe as well as globally. The EU response to the diversification and expansion of human trafficking, at least at European Commission level, has been to strengthen its commitment to partnership between its member states.

The UK's focus regarding sexual and labour exploitation has, however, shifted in a divergent direction to the EU since the election of the coalition government in 2010, potentially undermining partnerships with its European neighbours. Theresa May as home secretary and the then prime minister championed a revision of Britain's approach, re-categorising human trafficking alongside forced labour, servitude and slavery under the umbrella offence of modern slavery. Concerns have been raised, notably by anti-trafficking NGOs, about the Modern Slavery Act privileging a criminal justice response to modern slavery over the rights-based response to human trafficking emphasised by the Trafficking Protocol, the CoE Convention and the Trafficking Directive. More pragmatically, that the UK government, and potentially Australia and the US, should seek an alternative to the UN and EU approach to criminal exploitation may dilute or complicate the partnership approach that most practitioners consider essential to effectively address the crime and consequences of human trafficking.

The effectiveness of the response to human trafficking may also be affected by the UK's withdrawal from the EU. Whilst there remains the possibility of negotiating third-party alternatives to replace the collaborative benefits of institutions and mechanisms such as Europol, Eurojust, MLA, JITs, the EAW and SIS II, the brevity of the transition period works against a sustainable settlement being found before transition ends on 31 December 2020. That the UK has historically had a strong influence in formulating the EU's counter-trafficking strategy, as well as supplying a significant proportion of intelligence to the EU's counter-crime agencies, means that the potential unravelling of close cooperation will also have an influence on the capacity of the EU and EU member states to counter human trafficking, at least in the short-term.

Having investigated the four Ps' counter-trafficking framework—pursuit, protection, prevention and partnership—this short study has found some success, but also caveats, in the ways in which each element of the framework has been put into effect. Pursuing traffickers requires unanimity of purpose and collaboration. The Trafficking Protocol was a necessary spur to action. Yet, subsequent translation of the Protocol's intent, notably its tripartite 'process' approach, into national law has resulted in inconsistent interpretations of the definition of human trafficking that have sometimes undermined collaboration between jurisdictions. That said, the EU has certainly sought to develop a range of collaborative institutions and mechanisms to counter human trafficking. The protection of victims has also been sporadic. Efforts by the UNODC and OSCE to disseminate good practice and establish standard operating procedures and a common approach to the implementation of legislation have not always succeeded in overcoming discrete cultural responses to human trafficking. There is increasing evidence that common and accepted prevention methodologies, such as training and awareness-raising, may be perpetuating this variation in national approaches to counter-trafficking, although robust evaluation of these methodologies would allow more confident conclusions to be drawn. Finally, there is evidence that the key to successfully countering trafficking lies in partnership. However, recent trends including modern slavery replacing human trafficking as a prosecutable crime in some jurisdictions and the likely dilution of collaboration as a result of Brexit represent challenges to the partnership approach.

References

Anti-Trafficking Monitoring Group (2012), 'All Change: Preventing Trafficking in the UK', April. Available at https://www.amnesty.org.uk/files/all_change_report.pdf.

Anti-Trafficking Monitoring Group (2018), 'Before the Harm is Done: Examining the UK's response to the prevention of trafficking', September. Available at https://www.antislavery.org/wp-content/uploads/2018/09/Before-the-Harm-is-Done-report.pdf.

Anti-Trafficking Monitoring Group (2017), 'Brexit and the UK's fight against modern slavery', July. Available at https://www.antislavery.org/wp-content/uploads/2017/07/ATMG-Brexit-paper.pdf.

Aronowitz, A. (2017), *Human Trafficking*. Santa Barbara: ABC-CLIO.

Association of South-East Asian Nations (2010), *ASEAN Handbook on International Legal Cooperation in Trafficking in Persons Cases*. Jakarta: ASEAN.

Bales, K. (2002), 'The Social Psychology of Modern Slavery', Scientific American, April. Available at https://www.scientificamerican.com/article/the-social-psychology-of/.

Batsyukova, S. (2012), 'Human trafficking and human smuggling: similar nature, different concepts', *Studies of Changing Societies: Comparative and Interdisciplinary Focus* Vol. 1 No. 1.

Bhabha, J. and Zard, M. (2006), 'Human Smuggling and Trafficking: the good, the bad and the ugly', *Forced Migration Review* no. 25, May.

© The Author(s) 2020
S. Massey, G. Rankin, *Exploiting People for Profit*,
https://doi.org/10.1057/978-1-137-43413-5

Bosco F., Di Cortemiglia, V., and Serojitdinov, A. (2009), 'Human Trafficking Patterns' in Friesendorf, C. (ed.), *Strategies Against Human Trafficking: The Role of the Security Sector*, Vienna and Geneva: National Defence Academy and Austrian Ministry of Defence and Sports.

Brian, T., and Laczko, F. (2014), Fatal Journeys: Tracking Lives Lost during Migration, Geneva: IOM.

British Broadcasting Corporation (2019), 'Brexit: Governments agree plans to replace European Arrest Warrant', September. Available at https://www.bbc.co.uk/news/uk-northern-ireland-49576159.

Broad, R., and Turnbull, N. (2019), 'From Human Trafficking to Modern Slavery: The Development of Anti-Trafficking Policy in the UK', *European Journal on Criminal Policy and Research*, Vol. 25.

Bruckmuller, K and Schumann, S. (2012), 'Crime Control versus Social Work Approaches in the Context of the "3P" Paradigm: Prevention, Protection, Prosecution' in Perrin, B., Reichel, P. & Winterdyk, J. (eds.), *Human Trafficking: Exploring the International Nature, Concerns, and Complexities*, Boca Raton: CRC Press.

Buckland, B. (2009). 'Human Trafficking and Smuggling: Crossover and Overlap', in Friesendorf, C. (ed.), *Strategies Against Human Trafficking: The Role of the Security Sector*, Vienna and Geneva: National Defence Academy and Austrian Ministry of Defence and Sports.

Campbell, L. (2017), 'Beyond Brexit – Beyond Borders Mutual Assistance in Policing and Investigating Organised Crime', Durham University Centre for Criminal Law and Criminal Justice Discussion Paper, May. Available at http://borderpeople.info/site/wp-content/uploads/BrexitExecutiveSummary.pdf

Carrapico, H., Niehuss, A. & Berthélémy, C. (2018), *Brexit and Internal Security: Political and Legal Concerns on the Future UK-EU Relationship.* London: Palgrave Macmillan.

Chuang, J. (2017), 'Debt Bondage and "Self-Exploitation"' in Kotiswaran, P. (ed.), *Unsettling Paradigms, Revisiting the Law of Human Trafficking, Forced Labor and Modern Slavery Fifteen Years after the Palermo Trafficking Protocol.* Cambridge: CUP.

Chuang, J. (2014), 'Exploitation Creep and the Unmaking of Human Trafficking Law, *American Journal of International Law*, Vol. 108, No. 4.

Cockbain, E., and Bowers, K. (2019), 'Human trafficking for sex, labour and domestic servitude: how do key trafficking types compare and what are their predictors?', Crime, Law and Social Change, Vol. 72, No. 1.

Council of the European Union (2009), 'Action-Oriented Paper on strengthening the EU external dimension on action against trafficking in human beings; Towards Global EU Action against Trafficking in Human Beings', November. Available at https://ec.europa.eu/anti-trafficking/sites/antitrafficking/files/action_oriented_paper_on_actions_against_trafficking_en_1.pdf

Council of Europe (2019), 'Anti-trafficking day: Victims must have justice, including compensation', 17 October. Available at https://www.coe.int/en/web/anti-human-trafficking/-/anti-trafficking-day-victims-must-have-justice-including-compensation-says-council-of-europe-secretary-general.

Crown Prosecution Service (2019), 'Human Trafficking, Smuggling and Slavery', *Legal Guidance International and Organised Crime*, September 2019. Available at https://www.cps.gov.uk/legal-guidance/human-trafficking-smuggling-and-slavery.

Danziger R., Martens J., and Guajardo M., (2009), 'Human Trafficking & Migration Management' in Friesendorf, C. (ed.), Strategies Against Human Trafficking: The Role of the Security Sector, Vienna and Geneva: National Defence Academy and Austrian Ministry of Defence and Sports.

Davy, D. (2016), 'Anti–Human Trafficking Interventions: How Do We Know if They Are Working?' *American Journal of Evaluation*, Vol. 37, No. 4.

Deighton, A. (2019), 'Brexit Diplomacy: the Strange Case of Security and Defence', *Diplomatica*, Vol. 1, No. 1.

De Vries, I, Nickerson, C., Farrell, A., Wittmer-Wolfe, D., and Bouché, V. (2019), 'Anti-immigration sentiment and public opinion on human trafficking', *Crime, Law and Social Change*, Vol. 72, No. 1.

Directive 2011/36/EU (2011), 'Directive of The European Parliament and of the Council of 5 April 2011 on preventing and combating human trafficking and protecting its victims, and replacing Council Framework Decision 2002/629/JHA European Framework Directive'.

Dottridge, M. (2007), *Collateral Damage: The Impact of Anti-Trafficking Measures on Human Rights around the World*. Bangkok: Global Alliance Against Traffic in Women.

Dottridge, M. (2017), 'Eight reasons why we shouldn't use the term "modern slavery"', Open Democracy, October. Available at https://www.opendemocracy.net/en/beyond-trafficking-and-slavery/eight-reasons-why-we-shouldn-t-use-term-modern-slavery/.

Drew, S. (2009), *Human Trafficking-Human Rights*. London: Legal Action Group.

Dwyer, P., Lewis, H., Scullion, L., and Waite, L. (2011), 'Forced labour and UK immigration policy: status matters?' Joseph Rowntree Foundation programme paper, 13th October. Available at https://www.jrf.org.uk/report/forced-labour-and-uk-immigration-policy-status-matters.

Ellis, K. (2018), 'Contested vulnerability: A case study of girls in secure care', *Children and Youth Services Review*, No. 88.

Esser, L., and Dettmeijer-Vermeulen, C. (2016), 'The Prominent Role of National Judges in Interpreting the International Definition of Human Trafficking', *Anti-Trafficking Review*, No. 6.

European Commission (2017), 'Communication from the Commission to the European Parliament and the Council: Reporting on the follow-up to the EU Strategy towards the Eradication of trafficking in human beings and identifying further concrete actions', December. Available at https://ec.europa.eu/anti-trafficking/sites/antitrafficking/files/20171204_communication_reporting_on_follow-up_to_the_eu_strategy_towards_the_eradication_of_trafficking_in_human_beings.pdf.

European Commission (2012), 'The EU Strategy towards the Eradication of Trafficking in Human Beings 2012–2016', June. Available at https://ec.europa.eu/anti-trafficking/sites/antitrafficking/files/eu_strategy_towards_the_eradication_of_trafficking_in_human_beings_2012-2016_1.pdf.

European Commission (n.d.), 'Together Against Human Trafficking'. Available at https://ec.europa.eu/anti-trafficking/member-states_en.

European Institute for Gender Equality (2018), *Gender-specific measures in anti-trafficking actions*. Luxembourg: EU Publications Office.

Eurostat (2015), *Trafficking in Human Beings*. Luxemburg: Publications Office of the European Union.

Eurostat (2018), *Data Collection on the Trafficking in Human Beings*. Luxemburg: Publications Office of the European Union.

Farrell, A., Bouché, V., and Wolfe, D. (2019), 'Assessing the Impact of State Human Trafficking Legislation on Criminal Justice System Outcomes', *Law and Policy*, Vol. 42, No. 2.

Farrell, A., Owens, C., and McDevitt, J. (2013), 'New laws but few cases: understanding the challenges to the investigation and prosecution of human trafficking cases', *Crime, Law and Social Change*, Vol. 61, No. 2.

Farrell, A., and Pfeffer, R. (2014), 'Policing Human Trafficking: Cultural Blinders and Organizational Barriers', *Annals of the American Academy*, Vol. 653, May.

Ferrier, T., and Kaminsky, P. (2017), 'An industry built on human misery', June. Available at https://www.mindsglobalspotlight.com/2017/06/01/32072/global-spotlight-the-overview.

Focus on Labour Exploitation (2016), 'Access to Compensation for Victims of human trafficking', *FLEX Working Paper*, July.

Focus on Labour Exploitation (2019), *The Risks of Exploitation in Temporary Migration Programmes: A FLEX Response to the 2018 Immigration White Paper*. Available at https://www.labourexploitation.org/sites/default/files/publications/Report_Risks%20of%20Exploitation%20in%20TMPs_May%202019_Final.pdf.

Francis, B., Walby, S., Pattinson, B., Elliott, A., Hoti, V., Phoenix, J., Verrall, R. and Peelo, M. (2018). *Data collection on trafficking in human beings in the EU: Final report*. Luxembourg: European Commission.

Fouladvand, S., and Ward, T. (2019), 'Human Trafficking, Vulnerability and the State', *Journal of Criminal Law*, Vol. 83. No. 1.

Gallagher, A., and Holmes, P. (2008), 'Developing an Effective Criminal Justice Response to Human Trafficking', *International Criminal Justice Review*, Vol. 18 No. 3.

Gallagher, A. (2001), 'Human Rights and the New UN Protocols on Trafficking and Migrant Smuggling: A Preliminary Analysis', *Human Rights Quarterly*, Vol. 23, No. 4.

Gallagher, A. (2014), 'Submission to the Joint Committee on the Draft Modern Slavery Bill', March. Available at http://data.parliament.uk/writtenevidence/committeeevidence.svc/evidencedocument/draft-modern-slavery-bill-committee/draft-modern-slavery-bill/written/7406.pdf.

Gallagher, A (2015), 'Two Cheers for the Trafficking Protocol', *Anti-Trafficking Review*, Issue 4.

Global Slavery Index (2018), 'Modern Slavery: A Hidden, Everyday Problem'. Available at https://www.globalslaveryindex.org/.

Gregoriou, C., and Ras, I. (2018), 'Representations of Transnational Human Trafficking: A Critical Review', in Gregoriou, C. (ed.), *Representations of Transnational Human Trafficking: Present-day News Media, True Crime and Fiction*. Basingstoke: Palgrave Pivot.

Group of Experts on Action against Trafficking in Human Beings (2016), *Compendium of good practices on the implementation of the Council of Europe Convention on Action against Trafficking in Human Beings*. Strasbourg: GRETA/Council of Europe.

Guardian (2019a), Brexit: key strands of British policing 'in jeopardy' because of no-deal risk'. Available at https://www.theguardian.com/uk-news/2019/jul/27/nca-harvesting-eu-databases-owing-to-risk-of-no-deal-brexit.

Guardian (2019b), 'Net migration at lowest level since 2003, ONS says'. Available at https://www.theguardian.com/world/2019/nov/28/net-migration-from-eu-atlowest-level-since-2003-ons-figures-show.

Guardian (2020), 'Immigration rules post-Brexit could fuel modern slavery, say charities'. Available at https://www.theguardian.com/uk-news/2020/feb/21/immigration-rules-post-brexit-could-fuel-modern-slavery-say-charities.

Guardian (2017), 'Using security as Brexit bargaining chip is reckless and lacks credibility'. Available at https://www.theguardian.com/politics/2017/mar/30/using-security-as-brexit-bargaining-chip-is-reckless-and-lacks-credibility.

Her Majesty's Government (2020), 'The Future Relationship with the EU: The UK's Approach to Negotiations', February. Available at https://assets.publishing.service.gov.uk/government/uploads/system/uploads/attachment_data/file/868874/The_Future_Relationship_with_the_EU.pdf.

Hestia (2019), 'Underground Lives: Police responses to victims of modern slavery', March. Available at https://www.hestia.org/Handlers/Download.ashx?IDMF=952a9bfc-b57e-42f0-9ff3-6efcafb5db6f.

Holmes, L. (2009), 'Human Trafficking & Corruption: Triple Victimisation?' in Friesendorf, C. (ed.), *Strategies Against Human Trafficking: The Role of the Security Sector*, Vienna and Geneva: National Defence Academy and Austrian Ministry of Defence and Sports.

Haynes, D. (2007), '(Not) Found Chained to a Bed in a Brothel: Conceptual, Legal, and Procedural Failures to Fulfill the Promise of the Trafficking Victims Protection Act', *Georgetown Immigration Law Journal*, Vol. 21, No. 3.

Independent (2020), 'Children coerced into drug trafficking face cycle of exploitation due to failings in system, warns slavery tsar'. Available at https://www.independent.co.uk/news/uk/home-news/county-lines-slavery-child-trafficking-drugs-protection-sara-thornton-a9365906.html.

Independent (2019), 'Home Office to lift cap on 'inadequate' help for trafficking victims', 1 July. Available at https://www.independent.co.uk/news/uk/home-office-modern-slavery-support-human-trafficking-smugglers-a8982746.html.

Home Office (2017), 'A typology of modern slavery offences in the UK'. London: Home Office. Available at https://www.gov.uk/government/uploads/system/uploads/attachment_data/file/652652/typology-modern-slavery-offences-horr93.pdf.

Home Office (2018), 'The UK's future skills-based immigration system'. London: Home Office. Available at https://assets.publishing.service.gov.uk/government/uploads/system/uploads/attachment_data/fle/766465/The-UKs-future-skills-basedimmigration-system-print-ready.pdf.

Hopper, E., and Hidalgo, J. (2006), 'Invisible chains: Psychological coercion of human trafficking victims', *Intercultural Human Rights Law Review*, Vol. 1.

House of Lords European Union Committee (2018), 'Brexit: the proposed UK-EU security treaty', 18th Report of Session 2017-19, July 2018. Available at https://publications.parliament.uk/pa/ld201719/ldselect/ldeucom/164/16402.htm.

Hua, J., and Nigorizawa, H. (2010), 'US sex trafficking, women's human rights and the politics of representation', *International Feminist Journal of Politics*, Vol. 12, Nos. 3–4.

Human Trafficking Foundation (2017), 'Supporting Adult Survivors of Slavery to Facilitate Recovery and Reintegration and Prevent Re-exploitation', March. Available at http://www.humantraffickingfoundation.org/sites/default/files/Long%20term%20survivor%20support%20needs%20March%2017%202.pdf.

Inter-Agency Coordination Group against Trafficking in Persons (2012), *The International Legal Frameworks concerning Trafficking in Persons*. Vienna: ICAT

Inter-Agency Coordination Group against Trafficking in Persons (2014), *Preventing Trafficking in Persons by Addressing Demand*. Vienna: ICAT

International Labour Organisation (2009), *Forced Labour and Human Trafficking: Casebook of Court Decisions*. Geneva: ILO.

International Labour Organisation (ILO) and Walk Free Foundation (2017), *Global estimates of modern slavery: forced labour and forced marriage*. Geneva: ILO and Walk Free Foundation.

International Labour Organisation (2014), *Profits and Poverty: The Economics of Forced Labour*. Geneva: ILO.

International Organisation for Migration (2007), *Direct Assistance for Victims of Trafficking*. Geneva: IOM. Available at https://publications.iom.int/system/files/pdf/iom_handbook_assistance.pdf.

Kiss, L., and Zimmerman, C., (2019), 'Human trafficking and labor exploitation: Toward identifying, implementing, and evaluating effective responses', *PLoS Medical*, Vol. 16, No. 1.

Laczko, F. (2005), 'Introduction', in Laczko, F., and Gozdziak, E. *Data and Research on Human Trafficking: A Global Survey Offprint of the Special Issue of International Migration*. Geneva: IOM.

Lindsay, R., Kirkpatrick, A., and En Low, J. (2017), 'Hardly Soft Law: The Modern Slavery Act 2015 and the Trend Towards Mandatory Reporting on Human Rights', *Business Law International*, Vol. 18, No. 1.

Mantouvalou, V. (2018), 'The UK Modern Slavery Act 2015 Three Years On', *Modern Law Review*, Vol. 88, No. 6.

Massari, M. (2015), 'At the Edge of Europe: the phenomenon of Irregular Migration from Libya to Italy' in Massey, S. and Coluccello, S. (eds), *Eurafrican Migration: Legal, Economic and Social responses to Irregular Migration*. Basingstoke: Palgrave Pivot.

Menkel-Meadow, C., (2020), 'Uses and Abuses of Socio-Legal Studies' in Creutzfeldt, N., Mason, M., and McConnachie, K. (eds.), *Routledge Handbook of Socio-Legal Theory and Methods*. Abingdon: Routledge.

Messer, K. (2019), 'Financial Investigations: Combating Human Trafficking', *Anti-Money Laundering White Paper*, May. Available at http://files.acams.org/pdfs/2019/Karen-Messer-White-Paper.pdf?_ga=2.189475752.2081021004.1565346569-955199830.1565346569

Middleton, B., Antonopoulos G., Papanicolaou, G. (2019), 'The Financial Investigation of Human Trafficking in the UK: Legal and Practical Perspectives', *Journal of Criminal Law*, Vol. 83, No. 4.

Mo, C. (2018), 'Perceived Relative Deprivation and Risk: An Aspiration-Based Model of Human Trafficking Vulnerability', *Political Behavior*, Vol. 40, No. 1.

Moyle, L. (2019), 'Situating Vulnerability and Exploitation in Street-Level Drug Markets: Cuckooing, Commuting, and the "County Lines" Drug Supply Model', *Journal of Drug Issues*, Vol. 49, No. 4.

Muraszkiewicz, J. M. (2019), *Protecting Victims of Human Trafficking From Liability: The European Approach*. Cham: Springer International Publishing.

National Crime Agency (2019), 'National referral mechanism statistics – end of year summary 2018', 20th March. Available at https://www.nationalcrime-agency.gov.uk/who-we-are/publications/282-national-referral-mechanism-statistics-end-of-year-summary-2018/EOY18-MSHT%20NRM%20Annual%20Report%202018%20v1.0%20(1).pdf

New European (2018), 'Barnier: UK red lines mean no European Arrest Warrant'. Available at https://www.theneweuropean.co.uk/top-stories/michel-barnier-uk-red-lines-no-european-arrest-warrant-1-5567376.

Nieuwenhuys, C., and Pécoud, A. (2007), 'Human trafficking, information campaigns, and strategies of migration control', *American Behavioral Scientist*, No. 50.

Okech, D., Hansen, N., Howard, W., Anarfi, J. & Burns, A. (2018), 'Social Support, Dysfunctional Coping, and Community Reintegration as Predictors of PTSD Among Human Trafficking Survivors', *Behavioral Medicine*, Vol. 44, No. 3.

Oram, S. et al. (2016), 'Human Trafficking and Health: A Survey of Male and Female Survivors in England', *American Journal of Public Health*, Vol. 106, No. 6.

Organization for Security and Cooperation in Europe (2014), *National Referral Mechanisms: Joining Efforts to Protect the Rights of Trafficked Persons A Practical*

Handbook. Warsaw: OSCE Office for Democratic Institutions and Human Rights.

Organization for Security and Cooperation in Europe (2013a), 'Policy and legislative recommendations towards the effective implementation of the non-punishment provision with regard to victims of trafficking', April. Available at http://lastradainternational.org/lsidocs/Effective%20recommendation%20of%20the%20non-punishment%20provision.pdf.

Organization for Security and Cooperation in Europe (2013b), 'OSCE Resource Police Training Guide: Trafficking in Human Beings', SPMU Publication Series, Vol. 10.

Organization for Security and Cooperation in Europe (2011), 'Trafficking in Human Beings: Identification of Potential and Presumed Victims: a community policing approach', *SPMU Publication Series*, Vol. 12

Organization for Security and Cooperation in Europe (2019), *Uniform Guidelines for the Identification and Referral of Victims of Human Trafficking within the Migrant and Refugee Reception Framework in the OSCE Region*, Vienna: OSCE/Office of the Special Representative and Co-ordinator for Combating Trafficking in Human Beings. Available at https://www.osce.org/files/f/documents/2/4/413123_0.pdf

Palmiotto, M. (2014), *Combating Human Trafficking: A Multidisciplinary Approach*. Boca Ratan: CRC Press.

Parliament of the Commonwealth of Australia (2017), *Hidden in Plain Sight: An inquiry into establishing a Modern Slavery Act in Australia*. Canberra: Commonwealth of Australia. Available at https://parlinfo.aph.gov.au/parlInfo/download/committees/reportjnt/024102/toc_pdf/HiddeninPlainSight.pdf;fileType=application%2Fpdf.

Pearson, E. (2002), *Human traffic, human rights: redefining victim protection.* London: Anti-Slavery International. Available at http://www.antislavery.org/wp-content/uploads/2017/01/hum_traff_hum_rights_redef_vic_protec_final_full.pdf.

Pickering, S., and Ham, J. (2013), 'Hot Pants at the Border: Sorting Sex Work from Trafficking', *British Journal of Criminology*, Vol. 54, No. 1.

Politico (2016), 'Europol first in line for life after Brexit'. Available at https://www.politico.eu/article/europol-first-in-line-for-life-after-brexitvb-law-enforcement-rob-wainwright.

Pourmokhtari, N. (2015), 'Global Human Trafficking Unmasked', *Journal of Human Trafficking*, Vol. 1, No. 2.

Ratcliffe, J. (2008), 'Intelligence-Led Policing' in Wortley, R., Mazerolle, L., and Rombouts, S., *Environmental Criminology and Crime Analysis* (ed.). Cullompton: Willan.

Rijken, C. (2013), 'Trafficking in Human Beings for Labour Exploitation: Cooperation in an Integrated Approach', *European Journal of Crime, Criminal Law and Criminal Justice*, Vol. 21, No. 1.

Roberts, K. (2018), 'Life after Trafficking: A gap in UK's modern slavery efforts', *Anti-Trafficking Review*, No. 10. Available at http://www.antitraffickingreview.org/index.php/atrjournal/article/view/329.

Salt, J., and Stein, J. (1997), 'Migration as a Business: The Case of Trafficking', *International Migration*, Vol. 35, No. 4.

Schreier, F. (2009), 'Human trafficking, organised crime, and intelligence' in: Friesendorf, C. (ed.) *Strategies Against Human Trafficking: The Role of the Security Sector*. Vienna: National Defense Academy and Austrian Ministry of Defence and Sports.

Shelley, L. (2007), 'The rise and diversification of human smuggling and trafficking into the United States' in Thachuk, K. (ed.), *Transnational threats: Smuggling and trafficking in arms, drugs and human life*. Westport: Greenwood Publishing Group.

Shin, Y. J. (2017), *A Transnational Human Rights Approach to Human Trafficking: Empowering the Powerless*. Leiden: Brill.

Simeunovic-Patic, B., and Copic, S. (2010), 'Protection and Assistance to Victims of Human Trafficking in Serbia: Recent Developments', European Journal of Criminology, Vol. 7, No. 1.

Szablewska, N., Kubacki, K. (2018), 'Anti-Human Trafficking Campaigns: A Systematic Literature Review', *Social Marketing Quarterly*, Vol. 24, No. 2.

Tjaden, J., Morgenstern, S., Laczko, F. (2018), 'Evaluating the impact of information campaigns in the field of migration: A systematic review of the evidence, and practical guidance', *Central Mediterranean Route Thematic Report Series*, No. 1. Available at http://www.eapmigrationpanel.org/sites/default/files/evaluating_the_impact_of_information_campaigns_in_field_of_migration_iom_gmdac.pdf.

United Nations Office on Drugs and Crime (2013), 'Abuse of a position of vulnerability and other "means" within the definition of trafficking in persons', Issue Paper, April.

United Nations Office on Drugs and Crime (2009), *Anti-human trafficking manual for criminal justice practitioners*. Vienna: UNODC.

United Nations Office on Drugs and Crime (2018a), Global Study on Smuggling of Migrants. Vienna: UNODC.

United Nations Office on Drugs and Crime (2018b), *Global Report on Trafficking in Persons*. Vienna: UNODC.

United Nations Office on Drugs and Crime (2012a), 'Guidance Note on 'abuse of a position of vulnerability' as a means of trafficking in persons in Article 3 of the Protocol to Prevent, Suppress and Punish Trafficking in Persons, Especially Women and Children, supplementing the United Nations Convention against Transnational Organised Crime'. Available at https://www.unodc.org/documents/human-trafficking/2012/UNODC_2012_Guidance_Note_-_Abuse_of_a_Position_of_Vulnerability_E.pdf.

United Nations Office on Drugs and Crime (2012b) *International Framework for Action to Implement the Smuggling of Migrants Trafficking Protocol*. Vienna: UNODC.

United Nations Office on Drugs and Crime (n.d.), 'Human Trafficking Knowledge Portal'. Available at https://sherloc.unodc.org/cld/en/v3/htms/index.html.

United Nations Office on Drugs and Crime (2004a), *Legislative Guides for the Implementation of the UNTOC and Trafficking Protocols Thereto*. Vienna: UNODC.

United Nations Office on Drugs and Crime (2004b), *UN Convention Against Transnational Crime and the Trafficking Protocols Thereto*. Vienna: UNODC.

United Nations Office on Drugs and Crime (2015), 'The Concept of 'Exploitation' in the Trafficking in Persons Trafficking Protocol', *UNODC Issue Paper*. Available at https://www.unodc.org/documents/congress/background-information/Human_Trafficking/UNODC_2015_Issue_Paper_Exploitation.pdf.

United Nations Office on Drugs and Crime (2014a), *SOP Manual for Law Enforcement Personnel of the Central Asia countries on the cases related to human trafficking and smuggling of migrants*. Vienna: UNODC.

United Nations Office on Drugs and Crime (2014b), 'The Role of 'Consent' in the Trafficking in Persons Trafficking Protocol', *UNODC Issue Paper*. Available at https://www.unodc.org/documents/human-trafficking/2014/UNODC_2014_Issue_Paper_Consent.pdf.

United Nations Office on Drugs and Crime (2014c), *Global report on trafficking in persons*. Vienna: UNODC. Available at https://www.unodc.org/documents/data-and-analysis/glotip/GLOTIP_2014_full_report.pdf.

USAID (2010), *Trafficking of Adult Men in the Europe and Eurasia Region*, June. Available at http://lastradainternational.org/lsidocs/Trafficking%20of%20 Men%20Draft_final.pdf.

US Department of State (2019), *Trafficking in Persons Report*. Washington, DC: US Dept of State Publications. Available at https://www.state.gov/ reports/2019-trafficking-in-persons-report/.

Villacampo, C. and Torres, N. (2019), 'Human trafficking for criminal exploitation: Effects suffered by victims in their passage through the criminal justice system', *International Review of Victimology*, Vol. 25, No. 1.

Ventrella, M. (2018), 'Brexit and the Fight Against Human Trafficking: Actual Situation and Future Uncertainty', *Marmara Journal of European Studies*, Vol. 26, No.1.

Vogel, D., (2015), 'The Concept of Demand in the Context of Trafficking in Human Beings: Using contributions from economics in search of clarification' *DemandAT Working Paper*, No. 3, December. Available at https://www. demandat.eu/sites/default/files/DemandAT_WP3_Vogel_Economics_for_ Conceptual_Clarification_FINAL2.pdf.

Ward, T. and Fouladvand, S. (2018), 'Human Trafficking, Victims' Rights and Fair Trials', *Journal of Criminal Law*, Vol. 82, No. 2.

Weitzer, R. (2014), 'New Directions in Research on Human Trafficking', *Annals of the American Academy of Political and Social Science*, Vol. 653, No. 6.

Winterdyk, J., (2018), 'Combating (child) human trafficking: building capacity', *Oñati Sociolegal Series*, Vol. 8, No. 1.

Zimmerman C., and Kiss, L. (2017), 'Human trafficking and exploitation: A global health concern', *PLoS Medical*, Vol. 14, No. 11.

Index

© The Author(s) 2020
S. Massey, G. Rankin, *Exploiting People for Profit*,
https://doi.org/10.1057/978-1-137-43413-5